LITERARY NONFICTION
The Fourth Genre

STEPHEN MINOT
University of California, Riverside

Prentice
Hall

Upper Saddle River, New Jersey 07458

Library of Congress Cataloging-in-Publication Data

Minot, Stephen.
    Literary nonfiction : the fourth genre / by Stephen Minot. — 1st ed.
        p. cm.
    Includes index.
    ISBN 0-13-099180-5
    1. College readers. 2. English language—Rhetoric—Problems, exercises, etc. 3.
    Essay—Authorship—Problems, exercises, etc. 4. Creative writing—Problems, exercises,
    etc. 5. American essays. 6. Literary form. I. Title.

PE1417 .M53 2003
808'.0427—dc21

                                                                                    2002071592

Senior Acquisitions Editor: Carrie Brandon
Editorial Assistant: Jennifer Migueis
Production Editor: Maureen Benicasa
Production Assistant: Elizabeth Best
Copyeditor: Mary Louise Byrd
Prepress and Manufacturing Buyer: Sherry Lewis
Marketing Manager: Rachel Falk
Marketing Assistant: Christine Moodie
Text Permissions Specialist: Robyn Renahan
Cover Designer: Robert Farrar-Wagner
Cover Art: Virginia S. Minot

This book was set in 10/12 Palatino by The Clarinda Company
and was printed and bound by Courier Companies, Inc.
The cover was printed by Phoenix Color Corp.

For permission to use copyrighted material, grateful
acknowledgment is made to the copyright holders
on page 136, which is considered an extension
of this copyright page.

© 2003 by Pearson Education, Inc.
Upper Saddle River, New Jersey 07458

Printed in the United States of America
10 9 8 7 6 5 4 3 2 1

ISBN 0-13-099180-5

Pearson Education LTD., *London*
Pearson Education Australia PTY, Limited, *Sydney*
Pearson Education Singapore, Pte. Ltd
Pearson Education North Asia Ltd, *Hong Kong*
Pearson Education Canada, Ltd., *Toronto*
Pearson Educación de Mexico, S.A. de C.V.
Pearson Education—Japan, *Tokyo*
Pearson Education Malaysia, Pte. Ltd
Pearson Education, Upper Saddle River, New Jersey

To Ginny—
wife, artist,
and treasured partner

CONTENTS

PREFACE

This text had its inception at a national conference of writers. I sat in on a panel made up of widely published nonfiction writers, prepared to learn a thing or two. Before the readings, they discussed the genre. One of them said cheerfully, "Just what is creative nonfiction? Who knows? I guess it includes just about everything."

Everything? News items from the Associated Press? Annual reports from General Electric? Congressional committee reports? Legal briefs? The President's economic policy?

I wouldn't have minded if the statement had been made at a gathering of electrical engineers. They have their area of expertise and we writers have ours. But these panelists were writers. Experts. We came to hear them, pencils in hand. If electrical engineers were that careless about their trade, there would be fires all over town.

Clearly, a textbook was called for. The book, I decided, should explain why creative or literary nonfiction is different from utilitarian nonfiction. Significantly and definably different. That would be step one. The book should help students to examine literary nonfiction with the care it deserves. It should guide them in the art of close reading, their key to writing fresh and insightful literary nonfiction on their own.

My hope was to write an anti-textbook textbook. That is, a work that would persuade readers that the most effective study of literary nonfiction is literary nonfiction itself. Why write a book that challenges its own existence? Because not all students have mastered the art of close reading, and because without that rewarding and essential ability, they may find it difficult to improve their writing on their own.

There is a kissing-cousin relationship between this volume and my other textbook, *Three Genres: The Writing of Poetry, Fiction, and Drama*, also published by Prentice Hall. Or perhaps they are more like grandfather and grandson. *Three Genres* has been in print for close to 40 years and is now in its seventh edition. For a while I was tempted to include literary nonfiction in that text, replacing the drama section. But the demand for a nonfiction text seemed too great for such an amalgamation.

Here's the approach. Part One has eight chapters that define the genre, describing its various forms and giving advice on how to establish a focus and a sense of structure. There is an important chapter on literary aspects, those pleasurable elements generally ignored in utilitarian prose. Another chapter deals with ethical concerns: what is right by everyone's standards, what's in the gray zone, and what is just dead wrong and can land one in jail. The final chapter in this section deals with how to read. Why does this come last? Because it takes that long to persuade many readers that they're probably missing much of the subtly and beauty of literary writing.

Part Two includes 14 contemporary essays. They have been selected to illustrate different types of literary nonfiction, such as personal experience, the biographical sketch, opinion pieces, a sense of place, and the like. Eight of these essays are analyzed to help students see how the work approaches that kind of essay.

The other six essays are marked "For discussion." That means I have, with admirable restraint, kept quiet. My only guidance is a brief introduction entitled "What to look for." Students will have read one or two somewhat similar essays; now they are being asked to do their own analysis. I want to encourage students to read analytically on their own. Once they can do that, they will have the power and ability to discover their own unique voices.

Although I have been describing this text as if it were designed for classroom use only, I hope it will be useful for those many individuals who are not presently taking a course. For them, essays marked "For discussion" can be thought of as "For thoughtful examination." Those who keep literary journals will benefit from writing down their own analysis and insights.

The essays vary greatly. Some are the work of distinguished and widely published authors; others, as you can see in "Notes on Contributors," have not published widely. I want to assure students that it is possible to write effective and even publishable nonfiction at any age. In addition, some essays are fairly straightforward, and others make use of flashbacks and symbolic elements. Each essay, however, illustrates a particular type of literary nonfiction, and each has elements well worth studying.

The writers included here represent a variety of racial and ethnic backgrounds. Students should know that literary nonfiction provides a dual function for minorities. It can help to define the cultural heritage for fellow members, and it can explain those traditions and values to the larger community.

I have always enjoyed contact with instructors, students, and writers through e-mail. I hope to continue this tradition with readers of this text. My e-mail address is s.minot@juno.com. We are also preparing a Web site under the name of threegenres.com. Writers are a scattered tribe, especially in the United States, and we owe it to ourselves to create a virtual community through the Internet.

I owe special thanks to my wife, Virginia, whose artwork graces the cover of this text as well as that of the seventh edition of *Three Genres*. In addition, I am grateful for the enthusiasm and assistance of Carrie Brandon and Maureen Benicasa at Prentice Hall. Of the many individuals who nominated essays for this text, I am particularly grateful to my colleagues Chris Buckley and Tom Morton and also to Dick Dreselly of Brunswick, Maine. I look forward to hearing from those who use this text.

Stephen Minot
s.minot@juno.com

1

LITERARY NONFICTION:

What Makes It Distinctive?

What it is. Why it isn't fiction. How it differs from journalism. Contrasts with reports and scholarly writing. Popular misconceptions.

"Literary writing" and **"creative writing"** are used interchangeably. At first glance, the terms may seem too broad to be helpful. Surely all writing is "literary" in that it is presented in words and sentences. And all writing is "creative" since it requires some degree of imagination.

But these two phrases have taken on a particular meaning. They describe a **genre** that, while as old as literature itself, has blossomed with renewed popularity in the past 20 years. Many readers (and even some writers) are needlessly confused about how to define this genre. It's simpler than one might think. Literary nonfiction is distinguished by three basic characteristics: It is based on actual events, characters, and places; it is written with a special concern for language; and it tends to be more informal and personal than other types of nonfiction writing.

These three characteristics are important because they save a great deal of futile argument. They explain the difference between literary nonfiction and other types of prose writing, such as **fiction**, journalism, factual reports, and academic scholarship. They also help us to identify short works that are sometimes published as literary nonfiction but are actually no more than journal entries.

Why It Isn't Fiction

There is a definable line between literary nonfiction and **fiction**. True, some short stories and novels that draw heavily on actual events and characters seem like nonfiction. But the fiction writer's approach is significantly different. As a result, readers respond with different assumptions. No matter how fully the fiction writer has used actual events, characters, or places, he or she is in no way committed to sticking to those facts. Fiction writers almost always revise and alter details from experience or research to such a degree that in the end a reader can scarcely separate what was taken from life and what was invented. Actual events and characters may have been a starting point, but they are only a means to an end. The end is a good story.

The difference between fiction and literary nonfiction is essentially a matter of commitment: the fiction writer is committed to creating a work of art known as a story or a novel. Nothing else matters. Occasionally the material is created entirely from imagination; but more often it is made up of fragments from life. Fictional characters can and often are based on more than one model. A character may be given the hot temper of one person, the life style of another, and the political convictions of a third. The setting may be a composite of several places, and the actual events altered to meet the need of the work. The writer creates something entirely new, borrowing from the rubble of reality. Even when fiction writers use their friends and family as models, their loyalty is to the fictional creation.

Writers of literary or creative nonfiction, on the other hand, are faithful to actual people, places, and events. Such writers have the freedom to select what to emphasize and what to ignore, and they often reveal their own feelings, but they maintain a loyalty to those they describe or quote, to the setting, and to what really happened.

How It Differs from Journalism

Journalism stresses accuracy above all else. Reporters have been fired for creating fictional characters and pretending to quote from them.

Partly because of the emphasis on accuracy, the approach is generally less personal than that in literary nonfiction. News reporting traditionally doesn't reveal the emotions of the reporter. Even though newspapers now encourage reporters to open with a "soft" paragraph about how the event affected a participant or onlooker before turning to the facts, reporters are not free to express their own feelings or reactions. They can't write "I knew at once he was guilty," or "I felt sick to my stomach."

The style of journalism tends to be straightforward, essentially utilitarian. It does not generally use literary devices such as fresh and original **metaphors** or **prose rhythms**. It rarely if ever creates **symbolic** suggestions. It almost never indulges in wry **understatement** or **irony**. Generally speaking, journalism sticks to the facts.

Writers of literary nonfiction, on the other hand, tend to be more personal, sharing their reactions, opinions, and feelings; and they are usually more concerned with an interesting use of language. This doesn't mean decorating the work with needless **similes** and **metaphors** or adding a few symbolic details to make it sound elegant. But it does allow writers to suggest by implication more than they state. Often this means using **figurative language**, such as metaphors and similes.

Here, for example, is how a reporter might begin a local story.

> Mildred Gray of 238 Canal St. stared in disbelief as flames leapt from her apartment window three stories above her. The fire, of suspicious origin, broke out at 1:35 A.M., rousing some 23 residents, forcing them to the street. The fire department was not notified until 2:02.

If the event was described by a writer of literary nonfiction, it would probably be handled in a looser, more personal style, perhaps like this:

> I was stunned into silence when I first saw two dozen people on the street, some in bathrobes or wrapped in blankets, staring at flames leaping from their apartment house. My first reaction was rage: this was the very building the notorious landlord Harry Cutter had tried to burn the previous week. Why wasn't he being held in jail? Then, like someone waking from a dream, I realized that there were no fire trucks there. Where were they? "Hey," I cried over the crackling of flames, "Hasn't anyone called 911?"

Both pieces are factually accurate, but the literary nonfiction piece places the writer right in the scene, it expresses indignation ("Why wasn't he in jail?"), it contrasts the writer's initial reaction ("stunned into silence") with a sudden realization about the situation. The writer describes this with a **simile** ("like someone waking from a dream"). The style has become both more vivid and far more personal.

Each type of writing has its function. You read the newspaper essentially for facts; you read creative nonfiction with the hope you will be drawn into a new experience and share the writer's feelings as if they were your own.

Contrasts with Reports and Scholarly Writing

The great majority of nonfiction writing takes the form of reports and scholarly writing. Every corporation, research lab, university, and government agency—indeed, all institutions—turn out warehouses of such writing. Most of these documents are incredibly dull for those not involved. They are written for those in a particular field. They determine corporate policy, record scientific findings, and shape the policies of government at every level. Their function is utilitarian. They are valuable, but they are neither literary nor creative.

It's not likely you'll ever see an economic report from the U.S. Bureau of the Budget that ends with a conclusion like this:

> Although I am paid well to make economic predictions that sound assured, I sometimes feel a certain uneasiness. At the end of the day, relaxing in the quiet of my home, I wonder if I, like the Delphic Oracle, keep issuing these slightly ambiguous pronouncements without the slightest notion of what the future will hold.

And then there is academic research. It is often the most formal of all. There is still a tradition of never using the pronoun "I," even when presenting fervently felt convictions. It is also hampered by a growing trend toward specialized vocabularies devised by different critical schools. This limits the exchange of ideas and, more serious, tends to isolate critical theory from the general reading public.

Most writers of literary nonfiction prefer to reach a broader audience. As a result, their style tends to be more relaxed, sometimes closer to the spoken word. Personal feelings are not hidden behind barrier phrases like "And so the evidence appears to suggest that in many instances. . . ." The writer of literary nonfiction is free to write, "It's perfectly obvious that. . . ." There is real pleasure in expressing one's feelings directly and honestly and in sharing one's experience.

Popular Misconceptions

Literary nonfiction includes many approaches, and we will examine some of them in the next chapter. But it is a mistake to assume that there are no limits. One of the most common misconceptions is that any journal entry can, without extensive revision, be called creative nonfiction.

This is not to downgrade **journals**. Every writer will benefit from keeping one. Some (especially poets) like to use a bound volume of lined paper that can be carried about easily. You can jot down with pen or pencil (remember those?) stray thoughts, topics, reactions to what you are reading. Others keep a special file on their computer, sometimes reserving a particular time to write, such as early morning or the last thing at night. Unlike diaries, journals don't simply review the events of the day. Their entries tend to be less organized than that. They include reactions to friends, the day's events, the news, and especially one's reading.

Both the pleasure and the value of journal entries stem from the fact that they are informal, often fragmentary, badly spelled, and disorganized. They are for writers what a sketch book is for a painter. The entries are raw material that may or may not lead to literary work.

If you are serious about writing, your private journal is just that, private. Pulling an entry out and submitting it to friends, a class, or a publisher as if it were finished work is an imposition. By asking others to evaluate it or make suggestions at that stage, you are really asking them to do your work.

Journal entries often become a good base for a creative nonfiction piece, but first they have to be given a focus, a structure, and carefully reviewed for style. And proofread. Always that. A good work of creative nonfiction requires the same careful revision one would put into a short story or poem.

A second misconception is that creative nonfiction is the same as an editorial. Argumentative pieces, whether a newspaper editorial, a partisan magazine article, or a political pamphlet or article, are persuasive essays. They are primarily designed to change the reader's opinions. With some exceptions, they stress persuasion in the same way that journalism places a heavy emphasis on facts. Both are utilitarian writing.

Editorials rarely make interesting use of language. And they are almost never personal in tone. They tend to be abstract in that they stress ideas or proposals. Such writing is enormously important because it shapes opinions, but only occasionally does it take the form of creative nonfiction.

As we will see, however, it is possible to express opinions, even strong convictions, in works that are truly literary nonfiction. Such works draw on all three of the criteria I mentioned at the beginning of this chapter: they are based on actual events and people, not just abstract ideas; they are written with a heightened concern for language; and they are more personal than other types of nonfiction writing. We sense that there is a real person speaking to us, not just an editorial board or committee.

Finally, there is the misguided notion that there is no definable line between creative nonfiction and fiction based on fact. True, the border between the two can be foggy. It is easy to become uncertain with a piece that, say, focuses on actual historical characters but invents dialogue and thoughts. One can, however, differentiate the two by asking this: Is the writer's primary commitment to the people, places, and events described, or is his or her real intent to create a fictional work of art, using such material as a means to an end?

Authors are not always entirely honest about the nature of their own work, and reviewers frequently ignore these distinctions, but a conscientious reader can usually determine what type of writing it is.

A word of caution, however: Arguing about how to classify a published work can become tedious and unproductive. Far more important is the question of how you as a writer are going to approach a subject. "Loyalty" may seem like an odd word to use when describing an author's attitude toward a work in progress, but it is at the heart of nonfiction writing. When a writer feels an obligation to be true to actual people, events, and places while at the same time presenting his or own feelings honestly, the work will be literary nonfiction.

2

SIX BASIC FORMS OF LITERARY NONFICTION:

An Overview

Personal experience. The biographical sketch. Personal opinion. Reflection. A sense of place. A slice of history.

Personal Experience

By far the most common form of literary nonfiction is an essay based wholly or in part on personal experience. Sometimes the work deals with events that are far removed from what most of us have experienced: struggling with an exotic, life-threatening disease, playing professional football, being raised by a single blind parent, sailing around Antarctica alone. More often, personal experience essays provide insights into more familiar activities. The death of a close relative, for example, is all too common, but if it jolts a writer into realizing how ruthless and unnerving random chance can be, the essay can provide fresh insights. Arguing with a parent about what actually happened on a particular day years ago is not in itself unusual, but the incident can be truly insightful if the essay reveals how our emotional needs distort our memories in different ways.

Each of these themes is represented in the essays you will be reading in Part Two of this text. You don't have to do extraordinary things to find suitable subject matter. Drawing significance from familiar episodes can take an infinite number of forms.

The word **memoir** is occasionally used to describe all personal experience pieces, but more often it is limited to those works in which the writer recalls events from the distant past. Frequently this takes the form of an older writer remembering events from his or her childhood. The term is less appropriate for an essay about, say, working on a turkey farm the previous summer or the trials of illegally sheltering six dogs while living in a five-floor walkup apartment.

Personal experience can also serve as the basis for other types of literary nonfiction. Quite often it is the vehicle used to launch a piece that eventually becomes focused on a place. Many travel pieces, for example, blend the author's experience and reactions with what is fundamentally a picture of a foreign city.

The experiences of the writer can also be used when writing a biographical sketch such as an interview. It may be the surroundings, the author's reaction to the subject. The same is true of other types of literary nonfiction such as those concerned with a place or personal opinion. For clarity, however, it helps to limit the phrase "personal experience piece" to those essays in which the theme is primarily concerned with the writer.

Determining whether a work is truly a personal experience piece in this sense or whether the events are just a vehicle for introducing a different concern is a matter of **focus**. We'll return to that in Chapter 4. The point here is that it is important to ask just what your true interest is before planning a new work.

The Biographical Sketch

The biographical sketch is a broad category that covers a variety of approaches ranging from the formal portrait of an individual without mention of an interviewer to a very loose reminiscence that eventually reveals itself as a study of a particular person.

Fully developed biographies often fill a volume or two. There is a tendency in such cases for the author to keep a low profile or remain invisible. Lengthy biographies may include letters and interviews. Many are so concerned with presenting the facts in a straightforward, objective manner that they are not truly literary nonfiction.

Short biographical pieces, on the other hand, tend to be more personal and more concerned with the literary use of language. Because they necessarily have to focus on a specific aspect of the subject's life or **character**, they are better described as "sketches."

If the subject is a friend of the writer, that relationship is usually made clear. It may truly close, merely cordial, or charged with **ambivalence**, those contradictory feelings that are particularly common in family relationships. Such biographical sketches tend to make use of personal experience. If you are taking this route, be sure to decide which is your primary concern: you, the other character, or some aspect of the relationship. Again, this is a matter of **focus**, discussed in Chapter 4.

If, on the other hand, the subject is a stranger, the piece may be based either on an interview or, more distant still, research. With formal interviews, the writer often keeps a low profile. The piece may open with details about how the meeting was arranged, the surroundings, the attitude of the subject. But in the course of the interview itself, the writer has to be careful not to upstage the person who is the subject.

When writing about a historical figure, it is important to gather more material than you will ever use. If you rely too heavily on one source, you run the risk of being imitative.

Personal Opinion

In the first chapter I suggested that most editorials and partisan political articles are not truly literary nonfiction. They tend to be abstract and are rarely written with the attention to language that we expect in literary writing. But as soon as one combines opinion with personal feelings and experience, the treatment naturally becomes less abstract, the tone more informal, and the style less utilitarian. An editorial opposing the use of drugs by young people may be impassioned, but the language will probably be as straightforward as a driver-education textbook. If the same theme, however, is presented through the author's actual memory of what it is to recover from a heroin addiction, the tone will become personal and the writing is much more likely to take on power. As we will see, some of the most effective opinion pieces present their arguments by implication rather than direct assertion.

The same applies to opinion pieces that are presented through the experience of someone other than the writer. Biographical sketches provide an opportunity to dramatize strong opinions about politics, social issues, or even personal preferences such as the privacy of rural life or, conversely, the sociability available in city living. There is, of course, a temptation to make up a character or to combine several individuals into a composite person to press one's point, but that violates one of the primary tenets of literary nonfiction, a loyalty to the facts and circumstances surrounding the event or the person being described. Omission of certain details is marginal, but invention thrusts you into the realm of fiction.

Reflection

A reflective piece is usually less structured than an essay based on an opinion. As we will see from two samples in Chapter 14, reflective pieces may seem to meander on first reading. Their tone is often that of a thoughtful monologue.

In a good reflective essay, however, that apparent aimlessness is only an illusion. The various elements are actually working toward a **theme** that will be made clear toward the end. The writing may move from **image** to image, but each contributes to some insight or observation. In some cases, what appears to be a primary concern is actually a **symbol** for some abstract concern.

The entries in one's journal are often reflective, but this doesn't mean that they are literary nonfiction. Often they not only seem aimless, they are aimless, intentionally without direction. But even the most fragmentary entries written late at night may serve as the basis of what might become reflective literary writing. They may contain the seeds of a potentially fine work, but it takes time and loving care to transform a seed into a blossoming bush.

A Sense of Place

The fifth of these six types of literary nonfiction presents a verbal picture of a specific place. Travel pieces dominate this category. The fact that many newspapers devote an entire section to such articles at least once a week is an indication of how popular travel writing is. Those that are promotional pieces are far from literary nonfiction, but others are written with a personal touch and a literary sense of style.

Exotic places, ones rarely visited, are relatively easy to write about. Almost any aspect of Siberia's winter season or a weekend in the Central African Republic will attract armchair travelers. Just getting there may be a greater challenge than writing about it. But more accessible places are just as valuable for the writer. In fact, one's own neighborhood is a likely source for those with imagination, and it may lend itself to a literary treatment. The challenge is finding a fresh insight, an aspect that arouses interest. Here again, a personal experience may be the best way to highlight such an aspect.

In Chapter 15 you will be reading an essay about a section of rural Florida. The approach used is far from the hype repeated in countless pamphlets and publicity releases. Nor does it trash the state. Instead, it focuses on the dramatic contrast between beauty and very real dangers. To translate this into human terms, the author has chosen not just visual details but her own strong sense of **ambivalence**, an instable mix of love, wonder, revulsion, and high anxiety.

The other piece in Chapter 15 describes an isolated and almost abandoned town in Mississippi. Both its present appearance and its history are unique. The authors of these two pieces have selected accessible places as their subjects and focused on unique aspects.

If you plan to write about a specific area, a good way to start is to make a long list of details—not just the visual aspects but the smells and sounds as well. Then write a paragraph or so describing your honest feelings about the place. Pay special attention to mixed feelings. At that point, see if you can identify an aspect no one else has considered. Once you have identified those elements, you will be ready to share your view and your feelings with readers who have never been there.

A Slice of History

History provides a good source for literary nonfiction, but it is not as common as other subjects. This may be due to the fact that it is often a challenge to limit the topic to something that is manageable. In addition, a great many historical studies focus heavily on facts and avoid both the author's personal feelings and literary language.

It is possible, however, to write about historical events or figures in ways that are clearly literary. Subject matter ranges from recent events to those from the distant past. As a general rule, the farther back you go the more difficult it is to find a well-documented incident that is manageable. Perhaps because of this, short historical essays tend to focus on fairly recent events. Often they are blended with personal experience. In such cases, there may be no sharp line between a memoir and a historical piece. When an older writer recalls being let out of school to see the German dirigible *Hindenburg* pass overhead with its distinctive swastika on the tail, the recollection of a personal experience is blended almost equally with a historical event.

History can also be blended with aspects of society: the difference, for example, between the 1950s when "the numbers racket" was considered a serious crime and more recent times when the lottery is organized and advertised by government itself. Such pieces can be presented in neutral terms, not taking sides; or they can argue in favor or against such a development.

These six basic types of literary nonfiction demonstrate the extraordinary range of the genre. You will doubtless find works that suggest other approaches, but these are the most common. Keeping them in mind will help you to read nonfiction analytically and with greater insight. You will discover how often they are combined for greater effectiveness.

Recalling the six types will also help you when you begin writing a new piece. Where will your emphasis lie? Are you primarily concerned with an event that helped to shape you as a person, or are you more concerned in introducing your readers to someone else? Your choice. Do you want to highlight a particular personal opinion or conviction, or do you plan to explore the subject in a reflective way, inviting the reader to do the same? Is it a particular place that draws your attention, or are you more concerned with its history? If you ask these questions before you write your first draft, you will clarify your thinking and may also save yourself a great deal of rewriting.

3

PLUNGING IN:

Getting Started

Examine your own experiences. Consider the lives of others. Review your preferences and opinions. Let your mind wander. Revisit a particular place. Uncover a fragment of history.

Examine Your Own Experiences

It's no surprise that personal experience ranks high among writers of literary nonfiction. Precise details drawn from one's own life have authenticity. And, as we will see, even the most conventional life is a treasure house of interesting incidents waiting to be developed.

Don't be intimidated by those professional writers who have invested months or even years immersing themselves in some foreign culture, profession, or sport for the sake of an article or book. For now, leave it to others to live in a Tibetan monastery for a year or join the New York Mets for a week or befriend members of the Mafia for the sake of nonfiction work. If you are relatively new to writing, you probably don't have the time or the money to try that approach. Dwelling on such exploits will blind you to this important fact: there is no such thing as an uneventful life. You don't have to leave your desk to discover countless experiences that could be developed right now as literary nonfiction.

You won't discover such episodes, however, by staring at a blank sheet of paper or a computer screen. Inspiration is vastly overrated. You need to review your life experiences with some sense of direction. Here are areas well worth examining:

If you have had an unusual childhood or adolescence, you are in luck. Even if it was unpleasant at the time, it can provide the basis of highly effective nonfiction.

Oddly, some people are reluctant to share the more dramatic aspects of their lives. In some cases, this comes from a desire to blend in. Remind yourself, however, that ours is a country that thrives on multiculturalism. Readers like to share the great variety of our ethnic, religious, and social differences.

Indeed, personal nonfiction brings us together. If you have a unique background, share it with pride.

If, for example you came to this country as a refugee, you can be sure that your experiences will be fresh for most readers and will hold their interest even if the details are disturbing. If you were raised in a repressive commune or experienced deviant sexual preferences, you may be reticent about revealing such details in an autobiographical manner. But if you overcome your hesitation, your readers will be both sympathetic and concerned.

If, on the other hand, your life has been more conventional, look closely at those experiences that remain in your memory because they are vivid. Here are four areas to consider.

1. *Ceremonies.*   Recall weddings you may have attended, or funerals, graduations, birthday celebrations, family gatherings at holidays. Ignore the part that went according to plan. That's of no interest to you as a writer. Look for moments of awkwardness, uncertainty, even anger. What you want are the details everyone else would like to forget: your sister tripping on her way to the altar, your uncle getting drunk at Thanksgiving, your best friend's refusal to attend his own graduation. It's the rough edges of formal occasions that you're looking for.

2. *Role reversals.*   No one likes those times when the child has to act the parent to a father or mother. But such moments are apt to reveal hidden strengths or weaknesses. In a similar way, a younger sibling sometimes has to act as adviser to an older brother or sister. Situations like these are apt to evoke **ambivalent** feelings, the illogical fusing of disparate emotions like distaste and pleasure or compassion and resentment. Incongruous emotional reactions are often what differentiate a bland account and one that provides honest insights.

3. *Moments of sudden growth.*   With luck, we all mature from childhood to adolescence to middle age to senior status, but the process is not smooth. We acquire new abilities and new insights in spurts. Occasionally there are setbacks. Transitions can be joyful or painful. Feelgood films recount the endless ways falling in love can convert mean-spirited and selfish individuals into models of perfection, but leave that to Hollywood. Even though something similar may have happened to you, readers will associate your account with countless scripts. That doesn't mean that you have to be negative, however. Abject fear (a boating accident, a medical crisis, a near-fatal fire) can kick an individual into a new level of maturity. If something like that has happened to you, try to capture what it actually felt like. Don't glamorize it. Insincerity shows through.

   Sudden growth often springs from contact with someone else—a parent, a brother, a sister, a teacher, a cop, or a neighbor. And don't neglect those who become a negative influence—living evidence of what you don't ever want to become.

4. *Moments of high emotion.* Great joy, abject terror, and deep depression have one thing in common: intensity. Intensity makes them possible subjects for literary nonfiction. You need more than the moment of peak emotion, however. The reader wants to know what came before. How did it occur? And how did it affect you? A news item of how you were mugged is only a news item. Don't fall back on that clichéd summary, "It's an experience I'll never forget." It shaped you in some way, and you may have to probe a bit before you discover just how it did.

5. *Reversals of expectation.* We like to believe we can predict the future, but much of the time we are wrong. Everyone knows that putting on an amateur theatrical performance is stressful. It has become such an enduring Hollywood plot **formula** that it won't interest discerning readers of literary nonfiction. But if you are, for example, a stutterer, and you found that when you played a demanding role on the stage you were able speak without a hesitation for the first time in your life, that would make an excellent base for a personal-experience piece.

Reversals take many forms. Everyone knows how an unusually bright student is praised by teachers. But perhaps only you know from personal experience what it is to be taunted by classmates as "teacher's pet" or "nerd," isolated from your peers. This might lead you to detest the very teacher who admired you. These are circumstances in which assumptions about a situation are reversed, and that reversal is worth developing.

Popular as personal experience is as a base for literary nonfiction, it shares with all nonfiction writing one serious temptation: tinkering with the facts. The temptation is greater with autobiographical pieces than with any other type. When the material is personal, it is less likely that readers will detect deceptions. Remember, though, that in choosing literary nonfiction as a genre, your first loyalty is to the facts. You have a moral contract with your readers.

You may, of course, decide that the experience would have greater potential as fiction. Often this alternative is well worth considering. But if you plan to do that, start from scratch by transforming places, events, and characters (new names, altered characteristics). Weed out what doesn't contribute to the fiction and invent new material that does. If, on the other hand, you decide to stay with nonfiction, stick with the facts as they occurred. Let your memory, not invention, provide the details that will give your work vitality.

Consider the Lives of Others

Enough about you! Some of the best samples of literary nonfiction are focused on someone other than the author. If you are not used to this type of writing, start off with someone you know.

It may be that right from the start a particular aspect of your friend strikes you as worth developing. Consider contrasting characteristics. Perhaps she is popular and outgoing with her peers but awkward and shy with adults. Perhaps he is rough and loud when with his male friends but has a natural gift when it comes to dealing with young children.

If a **theme** doesn't occur to you, try conducting an informal interview. This is good practice for dealing with strangers. Try to avoid aimless conversation. The best way to stay on track is to make up a list of questions in advance, perhaps about schooling, interests, or plans for the future. After those fact-gathering questions, try more probing queries such as "If you had free time and money, what would you most like to do?" "What annoys you the most?" "What do you consider the best aspect of your personality?" "What aspect of yourself would you like to improve?"

Don't lock yourself into your prepared questions. If your respondent reveals something that sparks your interest, follow up on it. Be careful, also, not to comment on his or her answers. An interview is not a conversation. Keep looking for a dominant characteristic of that individual that will give the reader a sense of having actually met him or her.

Interviewing older people about their childhood can be rewarding, but there are special considerations you should keep in mind. First, when dealing with individuals who are very old, be very careful not to sound patronizing. If your respondent is not sure of English or was raised in a culture far removed from yours, it is all too easy to adopt the tone we sometimes use when asking questions of a child. You can show genuine interest without using saccharine phrases like, "That's *fascinating*," "that's a-*mazing*," and "you're ter-*ific*."

In addition, let your respondent wander or repeat material. It may take you a little more time, but remember that it often takes an older person a while to dredge up details from decades ago. If there are contradictions, don't comment on them directly. Return to that area later for clarification.

Interviewers vary on whether to use a tape recorder. A recording may help you to clarify details and reproduce actual phrasing when you write up the interview, but there are several disadvantages. The machine may intimidate some respondents, and changing diskettes in mid-interview can be distracting. I can assure you from experience that failing batteries can be even worse.

Perhaps the most serious liability to using a tape recorder is that a transcript may encourage you to quote too much and include repetitions in your written report. Some of the best nonfiction writers (Gay Talese, for one) never use a recorder, for just this reason.

When you turn to writing, remember that you are not reporting that individual's whole life. Full biographies require a full volume. What you are looking for is a particular aspect of that person's life. It can be an act of courage, a personality trait such as loyalty or insensitivity, a contrast between one period in his or her life and another, or a significant decision. Since you may not know in advance just what you are looking for, be prepared to gather more material than you will ever use.

Selecting the most interesting aspect of your respondent is a matter of **focus,** described in the next chapter. For now, keep in mind that the subject of your essay is not the individual, it is an *aspect* of that individual.

No matter who you are interviewing, keep these three principles in mind: Prepare your questions but don't be a slave to them. Show interest but don't introduce your own views. Unify your essay by focusing on a particular aspect of your respondent.

Review Your Preferences and Opinions

Most newspapers have an **Op-Ed** section. The term is an acronym for "opposite the editorial page." The letters to the editor in the Op-Ed section tend to be brief and are usually more concerned with opinion than style. They may represent deeply felt views, but they are not helpful models for literary nonfiction. The longer pieces vary; some are completely without literary merit, but others have characteristics of literary nonfiction.

As a general rule, the pieces that are essentially abstract arguments about political or economic issues are written without much attention to style. Their primary purpose is to win an argument. Such articles may be clear and well organized, but they lack what we have been calling **literary** or **creative** elements. On the other hand, those that make use of personal experience, case histories, or historical material are more likely to use literary techniques such as **metaphors, irony**, or implication, and techniques of **prose rhythm** (described in Chapter 6).

This distinction may seem subtle, but it becomes clearer when one deals with specific works. An essay arguing for an increase in the minimum wage, for example, may offer tables comparing the buying power of entry-level workers over the course of many years and make use of statistics comparing the rate of inflation to the buying power of manual laborers. Its style, will probably be no more creative than a lawn-mower instruction manual. Both the argumentative essay and the manual have a specific and utilitarian purpose, but neither is intended to give readers enough pleasure to return to it later.

A literary nonfiction piece, on the other hand, will usually humanize such a topic. Perhaps the subject is a single parent with three children who has stayed off welfare with a job plucking chickens but still can't manage to pay the rent and feed her kids. Or the author might interview three garment factory workers. The use of case histories won't automatically transform such essays into literary nonfiction, but the technique provides an opportunity to dramatize the topic and provide greater depth. If done with attention to style, the essay will go beyond the level of a straightforward argument and become literary nonfiction.

This distinction is seen in art as well. Some painters have expressed social and political views in their paintings. Jean François Millet, a 19th-century French painter, for example, portrayed agricultural workers in a way that emphasized the dark monotony of their lives, and the Spanish painter Goya used his art to attack the brutality of war. But we value their work for its artistic quality just as much as for its social or political message.

Political posters, on the other hand, emphasize the message more than artistic expression. Those that aid war efforts by portraying, say, Uncle Sam and cartoon images of the enemy serve a single purpose, to create patriotic fervor. Once that cause is over, the posters are torn down. They have served their purpose. Fully developed works of art are like literary nonfiction in that their value continues even after the political or social issues have faded.

Let Your Mind Wander

It is unlikely that you were encouraged to daydream in all your years of schooling. But if you want to plunge into writing, this may be one way to do it.

If you keep a journal, you will have collected many samples of mental grazing. It is a good idea to go through them from time to time the way you might go through an old photo album. As I pointed out before, the entries themselves are not likely to be even first drafts of literary nonfiction, but they may suggest a topic or at least a direction for exploration.

Even if you have not been keeping a journal, you can cast about for topics in a random manner. Write down the names of four people you admire and four you dislike. See if you can detect what it is that you look for in friends. Is there a reflective essay there?

Now select and describe briefly four periods of time in which you were really happy. Some may be social occasions, but don't forget times when you were alone or simply with one other person. It will help if you select different types of pleasure. Now do the same for four periods of time you hope you will never have to repeat. Next, look over your material and see if there are patterns you hadn't expected to find. What exactly is pleasure for you? This may result in some self-discovery, and describing what you have discovered may well be the beginning of a reflective essay.

A reflective essay may end up being an opinion piece or even an argument. Or it may take the form of a biographical sketch. But don't force it into a shape that doesn't seem appropriate or true to your own feelings. An observation about the way people interact or seek contentment can be in itself rewarding if the view is fresh and original.

Revisit a Particular Place

When you were in grade school you probably wrote essays about specific places entitled, "Egypt, A Land of Contrasts," "Puerto Rico, Statehood or Not?" and "Los Angeles, More Than Tinsel." You probably learned that the trick was to use two different sources and not to copy more than one complete sentence from either. This technique is a poor model for literary nonfiction.

Literary nonfiction articles describing a particular place are frequently presented through personal experience. There are good reasons for this. First, the personal approach helps to avoid the **clichés** of travel writers. True, your presence is no absolute safeguard against using those seventh-grade favorite phrases, "a land of contrasts" (which can be applied to just about any country, city, or town in the world) or "a place that time forgot" (that is, poor), or "a town that would not die" (melodrama with grit). But if you as a writer know the place personally, you are less likely to be tempted by time-worn generalities.

To put it in more positive terms, when you select a place you know well you have at your disposal thousands of details that can help to provide a sense of authenticity. The first step in any piece based on a particular place is to concentrate on the sights, the sounds, the smells that make that locality unique. If you have been there, you can draw on your own memory. If you haven't, you will have to borrow from other writers. Choose wisely.

There are two types of literary nonfiction pieces based on place. One type focuses on places known at least by reputation to most readers. These include travel articles written with care and a personal touch. They occasionally describe some aspect of an entire country, but much more often are limited to a specific region, a city, or even a portion of a city. Readers may never have been there, but they could identify such a place on a map.

The other type has a much narrower focus: a place well known to the writer but not known to those who do not live there. The author's hometown is a popular choice, but it can focus on a particular neighborhood, a mall, even a school yard.

No matter what the subject, **tone** is important. We'll return to tone in Chapter 6, but be aware that the same place can be treated with affection, wonder, bitter resentment, or even rage. Or the tone may be a mix of feelings. When we look back on our childhood neighborhood, for example, our sense of pleasure may be equally mixed with discontent.

As you search for a topic, review all the places you have been. Don't pretend to know a foreign country well if you were only a tourist there, but your experience as a short-term visitor may have real potential. As with all nonfiction, don't fake it. Use what you know.

If you have never lived anywhere but the town or city of your birth, don't assume that writing about place is not for you. Actually you possess a special advantage: you have an insider's knowledge of that spot. Your challenge is not a matter of finding material; it is to see vividly what has been so familiar to you. A good deal of nonfiction writing is learning how to see with fresh vision what you simply took for granted before you stated writing.

No matter whether you are dealing with a foreign country or the particulars of your neighborhood, keep an eye out for contrasts. Again, be careful to avoid clichés. The best way to do this is to find the details that will show the contrasts. Visual details, for example, will dramatize the contrast between the run-down commercial district of a city and an affluent suburban neighborhood nearby. Minor incidents will contrast the hostile nature of life on a particular city street as opposed to the sense of shelter once one is safely home. The smells and sounds recalled from a summer job in a slaughter-house might provide a sharp contrast with a weekend hike in the woods when the job was over.

To activate your memory, write down a list of the various places you have lived, leaving a space between each heading. Then fill in specific visual details you associate with each place. As you look over your notes, linger with each place and imagine someone asking you, "What was it like?" This is your reader speaking to you. Your answer will launch a nonfiction article.

Uncover a Fragment of History

Using historical material requires a ruthless process of reduction. No one (I hope) has to be told that "The Roman Empire" is no subject for a single essay. Cutting it down to "Julius Caesar" reduces it to those seventh-grade papers lifted so deftly from the National Geographic. If, however, you track down one of Julius Caesar's financial supporters who built a fortune by pro-viding fire protection to wealthy homeowners and letting the homes of oth-ers burn to the ground, you might be on to something.

There are a number of questions you should ask yourself before selecting a historical topic. First, is the incident narrow enough in scope to be described in a few pages? As the Julius Caesar example shows, finding a workable topic is like using a zoom lens, continually moving closer to very specific fragments of history.

Second, is it something that is not already known to the reading public? Shakespeare beat you to it describing the rise and fall of Julius Caesar, and even he took five acts to do so. Hunt for overlooked scraps of history.

Third, does the topic suggest some parallel with our own times or some connection with larger historical events? This isn't essential, but it adds an-other dimension. It may have occurred to you that our example of campaign financing in Caesar's time has a certain familiar ring.

In the search for historical topics, don't ignore fairly recent events. Some-thing that occurred 20 years ago may have a significant impact on our lives today. Frequently you will find yourself dealing with social issues. The closer the material is to the present, the more likely it is that you can develop a per-sonal connection. If, for example, you are considering the subject of drug use, consider giving your treatment a human dimension by including your own experience or those of people you have interviewed. If you are able to contrast shifts in attitude, your essay enters the area of historical nonfiction.

How do you find historical topics? Not by a hasty reading of a history book or by taking a survey course. Look for little details. When a historical event seems to suggest an interesting turn of events, you will have to spend time in the library or on the Internet to dig out the specifics. Perhaps for this reason, short historical topics are far less common than those based on personal expe-rience, but if you have a topic that seems promising, that time will be well spent.

No matter what direction you take in your search for a topic, make it an active search. Don't just brood; write down as many alternatives as you can. Start by listing the experiences that have had a lasting effect on your development. Make another list of people you know, friends or relatives, whose lives interest you. Consider asking one for an interview. Take a close look at your preferences and opinions. Then look over your journal entries or let your mind wander—though not for long. Revisit in your mind places you have been. And, finally, jot down some interesting fragment of history you might be able to research.

As soon as you find a topic that seems to have potential, you have a choice. Some writers prefer to work out a rough outline before they start their first draft. This can be particularly helpful if the essay promises to be fairly long. Others, however, like to jump right in, reserving matters of structure and emphasis for later drafts. This makes sense if the piece is to be relatively short.

In either case, remember that the rough draft is just that. After you have completed the draft, you will want to look closely at the **focus** of the work. Equally important, examine the **style**, the subject of Chapter 6.

One final word of advice: be careful not to allow excessive planning and uncertainty stand in the way of actually writing. There will be time to make both major and minor changes as you enter the revision stage. Right now it is important to launch your first draft with confidence and determination.

4

THEME:

What's Your Point?

Why theme is essential. When the theme shifts as you write. Outlining: for and against. Effective openings. Subtle closings. Making use of group discussions.

The **theme,** or **central concern,** of an essay is the principle statement or implication of the work. *Theme* is sometimes confused with **focus,** the primary subject matter of an essay. For example, the *focus* of the essay you will be reading in Chapter 15 is rural Florida, but the *theme* might be described as "Certain places are a dramatic mix of beauty and physical danger." The focus is generally a person, place, or event. Theme is what the author says or implies about the subject. It can be described as that abstract portion of a literary work that comments on the human condition.

It is important to describe the theme in one complete sentence. This is the best way to stay precise. While the theme of an essay, like that of a story, can be described in somewhat different ways by different readers, there should be a consensus. If three readers have totally different and unrelated notions about what the theme of an essay is, the work can be described as thematically confused. Saying that an essay (or a story) should mean all things to all readers is to say it has no meaning. To put it more bluntly, it is pointless.

Occasionally the theme of an essay can be perfectly clear to the author but not to readers. In such cases we say that the theme is fuzzy or blurred. If this happens to you, write out in a sentence or two what you feel the theme is and, setting that aside with your notes, devise one more revision. Increasing the clarity may be easier than you think. The theme of an essay should come through to any conscientious reader without your explanations.

It is a more serious problem when the theme is not clear in your own mind. In such cases, the revisions may have to be more extensive. Readers may be helpful in discussion, but don't ask them to do your work.

There may be times when you will want to start writing without knowing precisely what your central concern will be. Some writers recommend this approach. Suppose, for example, you went hiking with two friends and the memory of it remains with you. You may want to start writing about the event without knowing whether to emphasize what you learned from the experience (personal development), what you learned about one of your companions (a character sketch), the area itself (a travel piece), or why direct contact with nature is superior to learning about it through books or television (personal opinion). You may have to plunge ahead before you are sure just which is the most important to you.

Launching a piece without knowing where it will go is really a form of journal writing and may be a valuable first step. Like sailing without a course or compass, it may lead you to unexplored areas, or it can put you on the rocks. Fortunately, unsuccessful writing projects are never fatal.

It is not unusual to discover an insightful theme as you write. You may even wonder why you hadn't seen it at the beginning. If you're romantic by nature, you can call it a flash of inspiration; but a more rational notion is that while you think you are writing without plan or direction, a deeper level of your mind is sorting out what is really important. It is similar to when in conversation you say, "I never thought of this before, but. . . ." The thinking is going on in midsentence.

If this burst of insight doesn't come to you as you write, you will have to take a second look at what you have produced. Returning to our hiking example, you will have to ask yourself why this experience remained lodged in your memory while so many others have evaporated. Is it because your companion turned out to be a bigot? Is it because you discovered you preferred hiking alone to being with two nonstop talkers? Is it because it awoke a sense of anger against those who planned to construct a 400-unit housing development in this very valley?

Is a theme necessary? Almost always. Occasionally you read a good sample of literary nonfiction that is so well expressed or so moving that it doesn't seem to need a precise theme. But if you look closely, you will probably find that either knowingly or unknowingly the author has provided a theme.

Journal writing is an excellent way to experiment with different styles and explore feelings, but those entries usually lack a theme. If you plan to use one, you will have to ask yourself what kind of significance you can draw from the material.

Fiction can keep readers in the dark about theme longer than an essay can because it provides both characters and plot as lures. Things happen. But most nonfiction has little or no plot. The work may not be rooted in character either. If after a couple of pages of an essay the readers ask, "What's going on here?" the chances are they will stop reading.

The other reason theme is so important in literary nonfiction is that this is what gives the writing a durable quality. When we use the word *literary*, we imply that the work has qualities that make it more lasting than throw-away articles. One of the highest tributes a reader can offer about a work is, "I liked it so much I read it a second time." Or "I keep thinking about that essay of yours." We rarely say this about articles that appear in large-circulation magazines or in the Sunday supplement of the newspaper even though they may have been mildly entertaining or informative on first reading. There is nothing wrong with articles about a celebrity's trail of failed marriages or dogs that have saved their masters from certain death, but such work is the literary equivalent of fast food.

For nonfiction to be memorable, to be a work of literature, it has to have meaning that extends beyond the present. The reason we read Henry David Thoreau's *Walden Pond* or Abraham Lincoln's "Gettysburg Address" today is that the themes they developed remain relevant to our lives and our concerns. This is not to suggest that one should start out by writing something that will reach future generations. But unless you keep the goal of longevity in mind, your efforts are apt to remain on the level of quick entertainment.

The time to concern yourself about the theme of a new piece is after you have completed the first draft. Read it over as if you were a stranger. Ask yourself three fundamental questions about the theme of your work: "What exactly am I trying to say?" "Will a conscientious reader see what I have in mind?" And "Will someone want to read this more than once?"

When the Theme Shifts as You Write

As soon as you have completed your first draft, be sure to read over your opening and closing paragraphs. Do they apply to the same essay?

Suppose your essay is focused on a small town that for generations has been split between Lutherans and Roman Catholics. You describe the historical background of these two groups, areas of friction, and ways in which they worked together. But the last page veers off course with a description of how peaceful it was to fish on a little stream on the outskirts of town. What happened to the theme that seemed so securely established at the beginning of the essay?

Our daydreaming mind meanders that way, and so do many journal entries. No harm there. But literary nonfiction, as I have pointed out earlier, is not a journal entry or a letter to a friend even if it has been devised to resemble those forms. Because it is a literary work, it must have more structure. As soon as you shift from private writing to work you plan to share with a reading public, you are in a different league. Openings establish expectations, and the reader is going to be perplexed at best and possibly irritated if you fail to fulfill those expectations. Conscientious readers (teachers especially) may struggle to find some kind of symbolic suggestion in that description of the river at the end. It's natural to assume that there *must* be a connection. What a disappointment to discover that all it reveals is carelessness on the part of the writer!

If you discover this kind of fuzzy focus in your own work, it may seem at first like a disaster. But it could be a blessing of sorts. Look to see if there are two separate essays suggested by this split. If so, ask yourself what it was that drew you off course. You may have stumbled onto something fresh that has more potential than the original plan. If so, you have a lot of new writing to do, but the result will be clearer and more satisfying.

This kind of drift from the original theme is particularly common in interview essays. What began as a portrait of someone else may slide into one that is more concerned with how you were influenced by that individual. If your subject is an important part of your life—a parent, for example, a sibling, or a partner—what started out as a picture of that other person may turn out to be an examination of your own feelings. This shift in focus is the type that becomes apparent when you compare your opening paragraph with your ending.

Outlining: For and Against

The question of whether to outline an essay before writing the first draft is a hot topic. Both students and teachers have strong opinions. Common sense suggests that the decision should be made not on the basis of a rigid theory but on two simple factors: the preference of the writer and the nature of the essay.

Some writers find that a simple outline establishes an order that in the long run saves time. They argue that knowing where you are going is like having a road map. It is a safeguard against getting lost or ending up where you hadn't intended. The time spent composing an outline, they feel, is more than made up for by reducing the hours you have to spend on subsequent drafts to bring order and clarity to a meandering essay.

The counterargument is that outlining spoils spontaneity. Many teachers urge writers to begin writing as soon as the concept comes to mind. Reshaping can take place later in subsequent drafts. The result, they argue, is looser and more personal. This approach has had a certain vogue in the past few years, and some texts support it like a cause.

Before taking a rigid stance, however, try both approaches and see which seems right for you personally. After all, writers had personal preferences about how to organize their material long before the right-brain-versus-left-brain metaphor was invented.

In addition to determining your own preference, take a look at the nature of the essay you have in mind. Both the length and the type of work will influence your decision about outlining.

If your topic calls for a fairly lengthy treatment, an outline may serve you well. More than just length, the complexity of the organization is a factor. With opinion pieces, for example, you may find it helpful to list several points in favor of your position and decide in advance what would be the most effective order. Your outline will also indicate whether to strike down opposing views in a single passage or to space them out, presenting them in alternating paragraphs with your main argument.

The same is often true with historical topics. Suppose you are writing about the almost comic shift in men's attitude toward hats from the days in which even homeless men wore derbies or bowlers to the post-Kennedy years when going bareheaded even in snow and rain became almost mandatory. An outline may be very helpful to remind you about the historical sequence.

If a personal experience piece or a biographical sketch calls for flashbacks, or if a history piece moves back and forth between the past and present, you could save yourself hours of revisions by knowing where you are going from the start.

If, on the other hand, you are recalling a farm you visited as a child, you may want to let your memories pour out as naturally as they might in conversation. The writing itself may bring to mind details you thought you had forgotten—like looking over an old photo album. The same is true of reflective pieces in which you explore a topic with the informality of a conversation. It may be that you will move from image to image rather than event to event. In such work, spontaneity is indeed a premium. This doesn't mean that your final draft will lack structure. It just means that the structure will take shape in successive drafts rather than at the outset.

One final point about outlines. If you do use them, don't be a slave to them. If in the writing you find yourself veering off, the shift in direction may be well justified. Just be aware of the change so that either then or in future drafts you can add a transition.

Effective Openings

Your first paragraph is a crucial one. Not only does it announce the direction and possibly the tone of the work, it will determine whether your reader will stay with you. Remember that no one but your conscientious teacher and possibly your all-forgiving partner is obliged to go beyond an unpromising first paragraph.

No, this does not mean a formal introduction like those in some works of literary scholarship or scientific research. Stay clear of: "In this paper I will demonstrate how. . . ." Instead, try to give the reader a notion of the subject matter and the way in which you will present it. This allows you wide latitude. There is no one right approach. Here, however, are some sample openings that are likely to hold readers:

1. "You never know for sure how you will act in an emergency until you are caught in a burning building."

This starts with "you" to place the reader in the action. It generates a question in the reader's mind. And the subject matter is dramatically clear. This isn't going to be about the pleasures of quilting.

2. "My sister was one of the most bossy, obnoxious brats I have ever known. I miss her terribly."

Here is an opening that is charged with **ambivalence**—the melding of two apparently contradictory emotions. Right from the start you have an idea about what the theme is going to be, and you also know something about the tone. It promises to be some kind of lament, but it is going to stay clear of sentimentality. This is also a good example of a **dramatic question,** a mystery that seizes the attention of the reader. What happened to that sister? Did she move away or is she dead?

3. "My old neighborhood may look like any city slum to outsiders, but every time I go back I feel a sense of renewal. It reminds me of who I am."

This opening doesn't have the drama of the first example, but it generates interest because clearly it will blend both a sense of place and an honest expression of personal feelings. There is a contrast implicit here: the appearance of the neighborhood and the effect it has on the author.

4. "The *New York Times* coverage of the *Titanic* disaster in 1912 highlighted the toll of wealthy passengers, even though the majority of those who died were poor and unknown. I was not alone in treating that distortion of the facts as simply the bias of a class-conscious age. But not until the *Times'* ongoing tributes to the victims of the World Trade Center disaster in 2001 has any paper made a conscious attempt to treat all deaths with equal detail and respect."

This is clearly an essay dealing with history, and it is also presenting an opinion. We expect it will be documented with examples from that newspaper. In addition to factual reporting, there is an unmistakable personal involvement. "I was not alone" includes the author in a general misapprehension. We assume from that opening that the essay will to some degree describe how the writer came to change his or her mind. This is a subtle example of the subjectivity that often distinguishes literary nonfiction from straight journalism.

Notice also that the opening lines suggest a two-part theme. First, it will attempt to show a class bias in reporting until fairly recently; then it will suggest that a more democratic approach was adopted by the paper's tributes to the victims of the World Trade Center disaster. The topic is fresh and the tone is personal.

An opening that attracts readers is sometimes referred to as a **hook**. That term, though, is more often used in commercial writing where the reader may be viewed as a fish to be caught. I prefer the phrase **dramatic question** since it is neutral and includes the notion of sharing work with readers rather than outwitting them. Dramatic questions also can be used in the body of an essay, arousing interest periodically along the way.

Returning to opening paragraphs as a special challenge, notice that many of them imply a promise. Whether it is the prospect of learning what it is like to be caught in a burning building, or how one can love a bratty sister, these openings, like those in a majority of literary essays, suggest a kind of contract with the reader: stick with me and this is what I will give in return. When an essay fails to fulfill that promise, readers feel cheated.

Be careful, then, not to promise more than you can deliver. This is what sweeping generalizations do. Here are some openings that, if presented seriously, promise more than can be delivered: "Unless you have been brought up in the city, you have no idea what civilization is all about." "Willow Springs, Nebraska, is the most beautiful town in America." "The only way to appreciate nature is to go camping." Openings like these are intended to capture readers, but they are so strident that they tend to invite opposition from the start. Worse, like many television ads, they make claims that can never be fulfilled. They're hype.

Notice, however, that I am warning against them "if presented seriously." Any one of them might serve if your essay is comic, especially if you plan a comic reversal. If the comment about city living turns out to be a character sketch of someone who, though a lifelong resident of Chicago, hasn't a clue about what the city has to offer, the opening might be just right. Or if the assertion about the value of camping introduces a comic treatment of a disastrous weekend trip, that too might be the right way to start. Developing a comic or ironic tone is a subject I cover in Chapter 6. For now, just stay on guard against the opening that hits the reader with a serious but insupportable claim.

Subtle Closings

The challenge of concluding paragraphs is entirely different. You are no longer trying to catch the attention of the reader. No need for an attention-getting dramatic question at this point. No need, either, for one of those stock phrases like "And so, in conclusion. . . ." The goal here is not drama but subtlety.

Most problems with concluding paragraphs stem from insecurity. If you are not quite sure that you have done what you wanted to do in the body of the essay, there is a natural but unfortunate tendency to be overly explanatory at the end. If you find yourself reminding your readers that "There are three reasons why he remains on the police force in spite of everything. . . ," it means that you may not have defined those reasons clearly in the work itself.

Watch out, too, for the **hackneyed** ending such as, "I should have realized that you can't go home again." That phrase echoes the title of a novel by Thomas Wolfe and has been used too often to seem fresh. One can, however, revise a well-known phrase so as to give it new meaning.

The best guideline to follow for writing concluding paragraphs is this: keep it simple and keep it relevant. Often this is achieved by selecting a detail that comes out of the work itself, not some abstract summary of your theme.

One effective way to close a personal-experience essay is to end with a bit of action that implies a mood or a decision: "I took the next bus back without saying goodbye," for example, or "We walked on the beach looking, I suppose, like a couple too young to have problems." Others may end in dialogue that rounds out a relationship such as: "'Well,' I said, 'see you around.' 'Maybe,' she said." Or, on a more hopeful note, "So perhaps I'll take the job after all."

Opinion essays and reflective pieces pose more of a problem in some ways because it can be tempting to rephrase the theme needlessly. Some writers solve this by providing a personal note to keep from sounding stiff. "There are times when I lose my optimism, but whenever I see an indigent prisoner defended with vigor by a lawyer pro bono, my faith in the system is restored." Notice how the use of *I* and the admission of occasional doubt give a human touch to what might have a somewhat impersonal presentation.

Establishing a clear theme is a matter of balance. You don't want to highlight your intent so blatantly or repeatedly that you appear to be writing for a young audience. Yet at the same time you want to make sure that a conscientious reader will, by the end of the piece, perceive just what you have in mind.

If you are not in a writing class or a discussion group, the only way to make sure you have struck the right balance is to keep reading each draft over and over as if you were an objective stranger. Weed out the extraneous and make sure that the details that remain contribute.

Making Use of Group Discussions

If you are lucky enough to be in a group, make use of it. Some people dread having their work discussed by others, but it is one of the best ways to improve your abilities.

Resist the temptation to break into the discussion to explain what you intended your theme to be. You aren't there to defend your work or to win the group over. The value of the discussion is for you to learn what came through and what did not. The only way you can do this is to exercise great restraint by remaining silent until the discussion is finished. Ignore comments that don't seem to represent a consensus. The reader may have gone through your work hastily or have a personal agenda that has nothing to do with you. Don't even try to explain. If you enter into a debate, you will shut off discussion of your work.

The time to pay special attention, and perhaps even take notes, is when two or more readers express similar views. Even if they make negative comments, keep quiet and learn. Those are the criticisms you need to plan further revisions. By the time the discussion is over, you may be bursting to explain what your intent was. Go to it. But remember that the true value of the session is not your explanation but the group's reactions and suggestions. They can contribute a lot both to the improvement of the essay and to your development as a writer.

Finally, don't be disheartened by how many revisions you may have to go through. That's what it takes to create nonfiction that deserves to be called *literary*.

5

CREATING STRUCTURE

Creating scenes. Time sequences: chronological and nonchronological. Descriptions of a place: a history or a tour? Analysis and opinion: organizing ideas. Generating curiosity. Using dialogue for emphasis. Endings that announce themselves.

Although **scenes** in nonfiction are often less distinct than they are in fiction, they remain the basic unit. Without attention to scenes, a work will seem to ramble like the monologue of a nonstop talker.

The most clearly defined scenes are often found in works of personal experience. The organization process begins quite unconsciously. Just in the act of recalling an incident, we divide it into scenes. As we begin to write about it, that pattern often remains.

Suppose you are describing a medical crisis of a close friend. It would be natural to start with the initial symptoms and then turn to an early diagnosis by a physician. If that gave you both a false sense of relief, your own feelings of elation might constitute a scene. The next scene might be a trip to a specialist who presented a more serious diagnosis. Perhaps this was followed by a stay in a hospital. Then an operation with a period of anxious waiting. The final scene might be solid good news and your response.

These scenes may not all be units of action. Some, perhaps many, might take the form of reflection. And they will vary in length from a single paragraph to several.

If you find it helpful to outline a nonfiction work in advance, you can describe each of these units in a single phrase like an abbreviated version of the description I gave above. If, on the other hand, you prefer the more intuitive approach I described in the previous chapter, plunge in and write as if you were telling a story aloud. It will probably seem natural to present the key events in the order that they occurred.

Whether you worked from an outline or intuitively, stop when you have completed your first draft and take a close look at the scene construction. Ask yourself whether you have presented the scenes in the most effective sequence. Watch out for sections that don't contribute. A paragraph about your friend's cat, for example, may have to be cut. Mark those scenes that have been given too much detail. A needlessly detailed description of the doctor's office may slow the forward motion. Equally important, make sure you haven't left out some significant section such as your feelings when you received the good news at the end.

Scene construction in personal-experience accounts is usually based on events and tends to be as distinct as it is in fiction. But scenes are the basic unit in other types of nonfiction as well. If you are interviewing someone, for example, it is up to you as writer to decide which scenes to develop fully and which to cut down or ignore altogether. The sequence is also up to you. Remember that you are not a court stenographer recording every word in its original sequence. What was told to you by your respondent are the basic building blocks, but the order and the emphasis are up to you.

The more abstract a nonfiction piece is, the more it departs from fiction-like events. Works presenting an opinion or describing a historical event, for example, are likely to stress ideas more than incidents. What we have been calling "scenes" may take the form of "topics." Still, they are definable units that are fundamental in creating the structure of the work as a whole.

Time Sequences: Chronological or Nonchronological?

If you are working with a series of events that you or someone else experienced, it may seem at first that the best approach would be to present them in the order in which they occurred. Suppose you are interviewing a homeless man. The details he gives you might well be scattered, not following any particular order. As you look over your notes, your first inclination may be to reorder his responses so that they start at the beginning when, let's say, he had a job and a home. Your chronological order would then follow him through a series of personal crises and downward turns until he ended up living on the street.

This chronological approach has certain advantages. It has clarity and may help to explain how he ended up where he did. You have transformed what may have been a confusing set of comments given over several sessions into a straightforward sequence.

On the other hand, you may feel that this sequence seems like a case history, lacking in warmth. In addition, it may make the opening dull. Readers aren't going to be fascinated by a description of an apparently happy man with a good job, a wife, a dog, and a well-trimmed lawn.

To counter these two weaknesses, consider using a nonchronological order. You might start with his present state. Your first paragraph could begin with a description of what life is like trying to stay warm under newspapers, being hungry, and never sleeping without the fear of being attacked.

An opening like this would raise a question in the mind of the reader: How did he end up like this? It has potential as a **dramatic question**, seizing and holding the reader's attention. From there you could go back to the less dramatic but important description of his life when all was going well. This is called a **flashback**. Your narration would then trace his history through setbacks to the present, which is called **base time**. Starting and closing in base time while the body of the material is presented in one or more flashbacks is similar to what in fiction is called a **frame story**.

An even looser approach would echo the fragmentary sequence of your subject's narration. The sequence would probably not be a word-for-word transcript of what he said to you partly because of the length and also because the repetitions would be boring as he crossed and recrossed the same scenes. Oral histories, like many conversations, often repeat the same material. If we're polite, we put up with repetitions as listeners, but as readers we find them obtrusive and sometimes irritating. Still, your somewhat selective version of this scattered narration could give the flavor of a wandering monologue. Since you would not be making up anything, you would maintain your fidelity to the truth.

Descriptions of a Place: A History or a Tour?

When you write about a particular place or a historical event, much depends on how involved you as author are. If, for example, you have done some research on how a particular village grew to be a manufacturing town largely because of a mill that was built in 1900 and later abandoned, you may decide to present the historical events as they occurred, adopting the chronological approach. But suppose the town is the place where you were raised and your interest in its history began when you discovered the ruins of the old mill while hiking? That might make a lively, more personal opening, and the organization might follow the stages of your research in libraries like a detective putting together clues about the past. The structure in that case would be nonchronological, based on your discoveries rather than on the history of the place.

There is a third approach, one that is primarily visual. You can provide an effective structure by appearing to take your reader on a tour. You could start with a description of the river, then move up the bank to the ruins of the old mill, and finally turn to the Victorian homes of the mill owners on the high ground overlooking the town. As an alternative, you could begin with the elegant homes and work your way down. In either case, you are taking your reader on a visual tour, pointing out the sights along the way.

Occasionally, historical essays also focus on a particular place. If you are describing a particular Civil War battle or the beach on which Allied troops invaded Europe in World War II, the terrain may turn out to be as important as the battle itself. In such cases, one of your options is to organize the work around the physical surrounding rather than a time sequence.

Analysis and Opinion: Organizing Ideas

If your theme is primarily a personal opinion, the structure will probably be based less on events than on a sequence of ideas. The further you stray from your own experience, the more objective your work will become. Remember, though, that the opinion being expressed is yours. It's something you take seriously. The essay will be warmer and probably more memorable if you reveal something of yourself.

If you are decrying the use of national parklands for oil drilling, for example, you can rely heavily on public records; but if you have camped in one of the areas you are discussing, it would be effective to use your own experience as an opening. If your familiarity with the area is extensive, your experiences might even serve as the structure of the whole piece.

If the essay you are planning doesn't involve personal experience at all, it will have to be organized by ideas rather than events. You will have to decide in advance whether you are going to begin with your strongest argument and work down or reverse the process so as to end with what you hope will be the clincher. Even then, however, you can keep the work from being a utilitarian essay by developing the personal experiences that led you to the position you are supporting.

Generating Curiosity

Curiosity is the magnetic force that holds your reader to your work. The most effective way of generating that force is by creating a sequence of **dramatic questions**.

As I pointed out in the previous chapter, the term **hook** refers to a dramatic question that is posed in the very first paragraph. The trouble with that term is that it ignores the need to reactivate a reader's curiosity periodically throughout the work.

Suppose, for example, you are describing a trip to Montreal, Canada, in a particularly cold January. If this is to be a blend of personal experience and a travel piece, an effective opening might be an incident in which, after removing your gloves to unlock the car, you suddenly discover that your moist hand has become frozen to the door latch. What to do? No one is in sight to help, and if someone appeared how could they free you?

An opening like this provides a jolt—a painful one—that will grab most readers. But for all its effectiveness, it isn't going to hold readers once you solve the crisis.

After that opening, you can afford some less stressful details such as ways Canadians deal with cold weather in good spirit, but in a couple of pages you will need something else to capture the reader's interest. Perhaps it is an invitation to take part in a race across the broken ice of the St. Lawrence River in heavy wooden boats. Boating in January? Yes, they do it.

That will generate enough curiosity to sustain interest for as long as you want to stay with the incident. After such a lively scene, you can afford to insert a reflective section, perhaps pointing out how people everywhere are able not only to endure extremes in weather but to capitalize on them, often through sports.

Nonfiction, much like fiction, progresses through a series of surges. Dramatic questions provide the voltage, but reflective, analytical, or descriptive sections provide depth and insight.

There is a limit to how much drama you can pack into an essay. Frequently those that approach the limit are personal accounts of high-risk activities such as mountain climbing, solo sailing, and experiencing urban violence. There is no simple rule as to how much is too much, but there comes a point when most readers would agree that the piece is no longer literary nonfiction. It has turned into a simple, true experience adventure story. There is nothing reprehensible about such work. True accounts about exploration, combat, and death-defying exploits have entertained readers through the centuries. But when action itself has taken over, squeezing out deeper, more lasting themes and ignoring a sensitive use of language, the work has stepped into the entertainment area.

Literary nonfiction also entertains, but the reason we call it "literary" is that it has qualities that go beyond instant gratification. It invites rereading and will appeal to readers not yet born.

Using Dialogue for Emphasis

Dialogue in literary nonfiction can increase vividness and a sense of authenticity, aspects that we will turn to in the next chapter. But it can also serve in a way that is rarely considered: it can contribute to the structure.

Dialogue grabs attention. It is highlighted with a new paragraph indentation and creates the illusion of the spoken word. It nudges your narration in the direction of drama. Because of this intensity, it has the power to highlight a block of description almost as if it were in italics.

Here is a short scene that is essentially description:

> My Uncle Harry's house swarmed with dogs. Mongrels, mostly, they inhabited every room. Some lay in front of the refrigerator, demanding a toll every time you went for a snack; they occupied the best living-room chair and the couch. You couldn't even go to the bathroom without being watched by a couple of mutts. He seemed to love them all.

The visual details are all there, but where is Uncle Harry? The only reference to him is the last sentence, and that is only conjecture on the part of the writer.

One way to highlight that descriptive passage would be to cut the last line and look through your notes to see if you can find a direct quotation that could replace it. Reread that passage with this quotation replacing that last sentence.

> "I feel sorry," he told me, "for folks who have to live alone. I'm surrounded by family day and night."

How can quotations like this be used to shape the organization as a whole? If you have a number of them in your notes, you can insert them at regular intervals. They will affect the pace of your prose, subtly breaking it up into units in somewhat the same way that paragraphs do.

This technique is not always feasible, of course. Some topics do not involve other characters, especially opinion pieces. With historical work you may not be able to document what was actually said. Unless you want to slide into fiction, you can't fill in the blanks, much as you might be tempted. The types of writing that best lend themselves to dialogue are personal experience and portraits of others.

One way to study the way dialogue can be used to help structure a work of nonfiction is to glance quickly at a series of short pieces such as are found in any issue of the magazine *Creative Nonfiction*. You can pick out those that use dialogue almost instantly. When you find one, read it critically. See if the short quotations are used to create units like long paragraphs.

Endings That Announce Themselves

Composers of popular music have two ways of ending a recording. One signals a conclusion a couple of bars in advance, either through the music or through the lyrics. The other simply turns the volume down in what is called the *fade-out*. Writers have a similar choice, though a majority feel that the unannounced fade-out is also a bit of a cop-out.

Most nonfiction pieces dealing with a dramatic adventure have endings that announce themselves well in advance. The reader usually knows what the goal is, and regardless of whether or not the narrator succeeds, it's clear toward the end of the essay that the work is about to end. In an account about climbing a mountain, the reader assumes that the work is close to the end when the protagonist approaches the summit; in a description of what it is like to survive a hurricane or a tornado, the ending is announced when the crisis has passed. The same is true of works that describe a sports event.

There is a common problem in all essays of this nature, however. While readers can't predict the precise ending, they assume that it will be either victory or defeat. This makes the ending at least 50 percent predictable. The only solution is to have an outcome that is slightly different from what was expected. This may take the form of disappointment in victory for some reason, or some measure of satisfaction even in defeat. In such cases readers are well aware when they are approaching the conclusion of the work, but the ending has not been anticipated. Be careful, however, not to add such an ending to a nonfiction work without evidence. Stick to the facts.

Ending a historical piece may be more complicated. After all, history is continuous. It is you as writer who determines when to close the account. Suppose you have selected a particular military unit in the Civil War that was assigned the task of destroying a railroad line. The natural end, and the one the reader expects, is when they either succeed or fail. But suppose you as writer are fascinated at how they went on to destroy a village with no strategic value and then they themselves were all but decimated because of faulty maps. Those might be fascinating events, but unless the piece provides some hint in advance about how much of the campaign will be covered, the reader is going to expect the piece to end at the end of each crisis. Make sure that you inform the reader about the scope of your work at the beginning.

Ending an opinion piece is often the most challenging. On the one hand, you want to avoid the time-honored but wooden formula once taught in high schools, "In conclusion, then, it is clear that. . . ." And it is a form of redundancy to repeat the opening sentence in slightly revised form: "The music industry is shooting itself in the foot when it opposes. . . ." First decide where you plan to end the work, and then compose a final paragraph that highlights the theme from a slightly fresh vantage point. This may take the form of a quotation, a specific example, or a **rhetorical question**, one that is asked for effect.

What about the fade-out ending? To be fair, it is true that a few successful nonfiction works make it work. They are often a type described as **poetic** in that they evoke a feeling for, say, a place or a piece of music or a particular season. Such essays may do this by bringing to mind a number of images without a particular order. They are often highly subjective in that they stress feelings rather than events or ideas. Since there is almost no structure, they could be ended at the close of almost any paragraph.

If you are tempted by this approach, make sure that you aren't simply raiding your journal, selecting a dreamy entry, and giving it to readers with the hope that they will see more in it than you did.

Ending an evocative but structureless work takes considerable thought. For this reason, most writers prefer to create a clearer structure, one in which readers will recognize a thematic intent and will know when the piece draws to a close.

6

LITERARY CONCERNS:

Style, Tone, Suggestion

Elements of style: diction, syntax, and narrative modes. Varieties of tone: objective, personal, ironic, comic. Implication: similes, metaphors and symbols. Prose rhythms: repetition, sentence length, subject matter. Pleasure in language.

Utilitarian nonfiction has, or should have, one primary goal: clarity. Government reports, scientific articles, historical analysis, literary criticism—all are designed to inform. A high priority is placed on facts and logic. In order to inform, they have to be clear at least to the informed reader. Without clarity, they fail.

Literary nonfiction does more. In addition to informing, it reflects the feelings of the author, the emotions that in varying degrees make it a personal account. You can't achieve this goal with utilitarian language. Your writing has to convey subtle reactions and responses to the subject regardless of whether that subject is a person, a place, an event, or a conviction. To earn the title of *"literary,"* it must communicate not only direct meanings but **overtones**, shadings of meaning. And in addition, the language should give pleasure in itself as music does.

Demanding? Of course. But that is the difference between utilitarian prose and literary nonfiction.

Elements of Style

Style is the manner in which a work is written. The same subject can be written in an infinite number of styles.

Some aspects of style are determined quite unconsciously. The great majority, however, stem from conscious decisions. They are determined by the choice of words used (**diction**), the length and type of sentences (**syntax**), and the relative use of description, reflection, dialogue, and action (**narrative modes**).

If you think too much about style when writing a first draft, you'll never finish your first paragraph. It will be like analyzing how a bowknot works as you try to tie your shoes. The time to examine your style is after your first draft is safely on paper or on the computer screen with a backup. That's when you read your work through as if you were a firm but kindly critic and examine the style.

Start with **diction**. Take a close look at the words you chose. Remember that English is an enormous language. It offers you many more words than you would have writing in Spanish, French, or German. Often you have a choice of two or even three words that mean *almost* the same thing. Technically such words are **synonyms**, but almost never do they have exactly the same meaning.

Dictionary definitions and vocabulary-building programs list synonyms, but they do a poor job of describing the differences between the paired words. These differences come from the **overtones**, or implied shadings of meaning. We pick them up quite unconsciously through our reading. This is why those who read a great deal have an easier time of writing effectively than those who do not.

Here are three sentences that say essentially the same thing but strike the reader differently because the key words have quite different overtones.

1. The young man struck the person in the abdomen and hailed a police officer while bystanders silently watched.
2. The boy hit the man in the stomach and called a policeman while onlookers stood by, speechless.
3. The kid punched the guy right in the gut and yelled for a cop while the crowd gawked.

It's all in English, and the incident is clearly the same; but each of the three versions uses different nouns and different verbs as well. No wonder learning the language is difficult!

Take a close look at how these three examples differ. The first is the most formal. It will strike most readers as a bit stiff, even stilted, though the meaning is clear enough. The third is at the opposite extreme. It is highly informal. By *informal* we mean closer to the spoken word. There is no slang here. ("*Gut*" is informal, not true slang.)

Informal diction like this makes the third passage inappropriate for a newspaper article or police report, but it might be just right as dialogue in a literary nonfiction piece. "Literary," remember, doesn't mean elegant or formal; it does mean language that is appropriate for a particular piece.

The second version is what is sometimes called **neutral style**. It is neither unmistakably formal nor conversational. It does, however, have style. Like fingerprints, every sample of writing has its own special characteristics. By *neutral* we simply mean unobtrusive. A majority of nonfiction works adopts this approach.

Diction, then, is a major factor determining the *level of usage*, formal, informal, or neutral. When you reexamine the words you have used in a completed first draft, make sure they are appropriate for the effect you are trying to achieve.

Syntax is the second element in the creation of style. Sentence structure varies not only in length but also in complexity. Here are two samples that use the same words but create an entirely different effect.

1. Biloxi, a sleepy town on the Gulf of Mexico, attracts tourists and retirees who are drawn to its old-world charm, its spectacular beaches, and its quiet. For me, however, born there many years ago, it was a backwater, a prison camp designed to drain all my energy and sense of adventure.

2. Biloxi sleeps on the Gulf of Mexico. Tourists go there. They talk about old-world charm. And beaches. They like the quiet. Retirees die there. For me as a child it was a backwater. It was a prison camp. It was designed to drain me of energy and sense of adventure.

The first version contains only two sentences. They are fairly long, and each is broken up with commas. The second presents the same material in nine short sentences. There are no phrases that require commas. "And beaches" is not even a complete sentence, but the meaning is clear, and the fragment is not obtrusive because of the informality of the style.

In general, long, complex sentences slow the pace and create a certain sense of formality. Short sentences with occasional sentence fragments have the feel of spoken language, but they also have the liability of creating monotony, especially in longer works. To avoid this risk, vary the length of your sentences, using brief ones for emphasis.

The balance of **narrative modes** is another factor that influences style. The narrative modes used most often in creative nonfiction are description, thoughts, dialogue, and action.

Description often dominates travel pieces. Unless you are careful, it can slow the pace. In order to keep your description lively, make sure that the details you use are fresh and vivid. As much as possible, avoid adjectives. Commercial travel pieces are often clotted with modifiers like "beautiful," "majestic," "unspoiled," and "impressive." If you concentrate on nouns, actual details, you won't have to fall back on overused adjectives.

Thoughts, the second narrative mode, often dominate reflective pieces. They are apt to move from image to image. They may appear to wander without direction, but make sure that beneath this appearance there is a forward motion. Otherwise what you hoped would be a literary reflective piece may resemble a structureless journal entry.

Dialogue and *action* are the most dynamic of the narrative modes. They add voltage to your style. Dialogue is most common in biographical sketches, but quoting others can also enliven travel pieces and works based on contemporary history. Action is at the heart of many personal-experience works, but make sure that it doesn't take over. The style of high adventure pieces can be described as superficial if the action is not supplemented with thematic implications.

To a large degree, the balance of narrative modes will be determined by the material you have to work with. You can't invent material just for variety.

But there may be times when you can make a significant difference to your style and the overall effect of your essay by making use of a mode you had previously ignored.

How do you improve your ability to write with an effective style? Mainly by reading. The more you read, the more unconscious stylistic decisions become. One way to speed the process is to read the first three pages of a large number of literary nonfiction works. After each one, jot down a couple of sentences about style. Make a note if the author has used colloquial phrases or remained fairly formal, whether the sentences tend to be long and complex or simple, and which of the narrative modes dominates the work. By reading only a portion of each essay you won't start thinking about the subject matter. You will keep focusing on style. Works in print are your best teachers.

Varieties of Tone

In some respects, the **tone** of a written work is like a tone of voice. A speaking voice reveals the attitude or emotions of the one who is talking; although reading is normally silent, the literary tone reveals the writer's attitude or feelings about the work.

Take a close look at the following statements about a writer's brother. Imagine that each is the first line of a biographical sketch. Although they all deal with the same person, each is written with a different tone:

1. My brother earns a good living designing computer games.
2. My kid brother is the star of the family thanks to his hard-earned success in designing computer games.
3. While the rest of us try to better the world in some small way, my brother rakes in an obscene salary fooling around with mindless computer games.
4. My brother has found life's highest calling by leaving the ministry and committing himself wholly, even reverently, to the creation of the world's most violent computer games.

The first sentence is an objective statement of fact. There is no indication of how the writer feels about his brother. The tone is neutral. The second, however, implies a warm relationship. The phrase "kid brother" suggests affection. He is described not only as "the star of the family" but as one whose efforts are "hard-earned." One of the differences, remember, between utilitarian nonfiction such as a factual report and literary nonfiction is the introduction of a personal relationship between writer and subject.

But that relationship need not necessarily be warm and supportive. In the third version the brother "rakes in" money, a phrase borrowed from gambling halls, his salary is "obscene," his work is described as mere "fooling around," and what he produces is "mindless." All it takes is a few nasty implications to establish an entirely different tone.

Something quite different happens in the fourth version. The description of the brother is cast as if it were high praise, but the intent is clearly just the opposite. The tone here is **ironic**. It starts out with the phrase "life's highest calling," but by the end of that sentence you know that this is not to be taken literally. It is to be read as irony. And not very subtle irony at that.

When irony is hostile like this, it is similar to sarcasm. But irony can also take the form of a reversal of expectations that may not be critical at all. An account about how an otherwise deadly blizzard drew a family together for the first time could emphasize that reversal of expectation. If the bitter cold of the storm were contrasted with the warmth of their newfound affection, the reader might well pick up the ironic contrast.

The objective tone of the first passage is what reporters, historians, and scientists strive to achieve. A warmer tone is achieved as soon as the writer adds some type of personal involvement. Most literary nonfiction reflects the author's feelings to some degree either directly or by implication. And irony reverses the literal statement which, when blunt and hostile, is called *sarcasm*. Irony, however, can be so subtle that the reader has to look closely to make sure which attitude is intended.

Implication: Similes, Metaphors, and Symbols

Similes, **metaphors**, and **symbols** have one thing in common: they expand meaning. There is an unfortunate tendency to think of them as decorations added to dress up a passage, but this is not so. Thinking of them that way will make your writing seem self-consciously "poetic" or "literary" in the worst sense of both words.

Similes and metaphors, both called **figures of speech**, are fundamentally comparisons. They usually compare an **abstract** concept to something **concrete**—an object we can see, feel, hear, taste, or even smell. Abstractions are hard to grasp because they are ideas. You can't see them, weigh them, taste them, or hear them. But they are enormously important. So we keep describing their attributes in terms of solid or **concrete** objects.

Peace is an important abstraction, but to grasp it we regularly compare it with a dove. This comparison has become so well known it is referred to as a *public image* (see **symbol**) and is used in cartoons. Writers have to find fresh and original comparisons to make an impact. For example, liberty might be compared with a sunrise or a wild horse.

To see how you can translate abstract feelings through similes, metaphors, and symbols, imagine a personal essay that describes an author's lengthy treatment for cancer and final recovery through surgery. What is the most effective way to communicate the sense of joy she felt at the end of that ordeal?

One way would be to use a **simile**: "I was too weak to move, lying there in the hospital, yet I felt like some kid romping with a puppy." The child is being introduced merely as a way of describing the author's mood.

A second approach would be to use a **metaphor** like this: "Suddenly I was transformed from a candidate for death to a kid romping with her pet dog." Transformed? We know that the writer doesn't mean that literally. She is using the child **figuratively**. Hence the term **figure of speech**.

Symbols work in a different way. The symbolic object is not something introduced merely for comparison; it is an item that is already a part of the essay. The writer gives the object an expanded meaning by implying that it also suggests something larger.

Suppose the author in this hypothetical essay ended the piece this way: "Before I drifted off to sleep, I managed to turn and see the hospital lawn below me. There was no one about except for a small girl playing with a puppy, the two of them rolling over and over in the green grass."

As readers, we would not say, "What kid? Where did she come from?" In the context of the essay we as readers could be encouraged to see the girl as a visual representation of the author's feeling of joy and her hope of renewed good health. The child is not a figure of speech; she really is out there on the lawn. But she is being used symbolically.

There are many **public symbols** that are so well known that they appear in cartoons—the image of Uncle Sam, the Russian bear, the old man with a scythe suggesting death. But literary works use what is sometimes called **private symbols**. A better phrase would be "unique symbols" because they are devised by an author and normally used only once. They are fresh and provide insightful associations.

Figures of speech and symbols are used less frequently in literary nonfiction than they are in poetry, but they are a valuable way of adding richness to your style. When you come across such a detail in published work, don't just skip over it like a speed reader. Stop, mark it, and identify the various overtones implied.

If you do use figurative language, be careful not to produce a simile or metaphor that is so lengthy or contrived that it draws attention to itself. For some unaccountable reason, this is a characteristic of commercially inspired detective fiction. If you are describing a moment of stage fright before a dance performance, for example, don't let your simile take over as in, "I felt as if I were clinging by one hand to a frayed rope, suspended over a pack of snarling, leaping, underfed pit bulls." Unless you are striving for a comic effect, avoid show-off similes and metaphors. In this case, "I felt rocks grinding in my stomach" would do.

Symbols can present a slightly different problem: obviousness. It is easy to avoid public symbols, but watch out for those that seem just a bit familiar. Even if after interviewing an older couple in a park you see the two of them head home, walking slowly into what is really a setting sun, resist the temptation to use that detail. Life can be corny, but your writing can't be.

The basic guideline to keep in mind: if you are going to use figurative language or symbolic suggestions, make sure they are subtle and original. Remember that their function is to enrich the essay, not to showcase the author.

Prose Rhythms

We associate rhythm with song, dance, and poetry. But prose can be rhythmical as well.

Repetition is the most powerful method of creating rhythm. Careless redundancy weakens style, but an intentional repetition has the effect of underlining a key phrase. We hear it most frequently in oratory, especially in sermons. Martin Luther King, Jr., was a master of this. It is almost as effective when written on the page. This technique lends itself best to opinion pieces since they are often organized by a series of ideas rather than events.

There is something compelling about a significant phrase reiterated as in, "It is wrong to assume that. . . . It is wrong to assume that. . . . It is wrong to assume that. . . ." A more positive series might be bound together by repeating the phrase "There is hope in. . . . There is hope in. . . ."

Sometimes repetition takes the form of a **rhetorical question**. These are questions that are presented for effect rather than with the expectation of a considered answer. In most cases the answer is assumed as in: "Do we want more domestic violence? . . . Do we want more gang violence? . . . Do we want to generate more war between nations?" The presumed answer is "No," and the slight variation in wording provides a sense of direction to the argument.

The greatest strength of repetition is also its greatest weakness. (Note, by the way, the subtle repetition in that sentence.) Repeating key words or phrases is a stylistic sledgehammer. It draws attention to itself, and if used too much may make your writing seem heavy-handed at best or belligerent at worst. Handle with care.

The previous paragraph suggests a second and more subtle technique of creating prose rhythm: sentence length. Ending a paragraph with a short sentence after a series of longer ones highlights that paragraph as if you circled it. If you repeat that technique, you create a rhythm of paragraphs.

Finally, paragraphs themselves can be used to establish a rhythm. This can be achieved not only by length but by content. Suppose you are writing an opinion piece describing why you chose a small liberal arts college rather than a university. The way you organize your material could establish a rhythm. If you alternate between the advantages of one as opposed to the disadvantages of the other, you will establish a rhythm in the work as a whole more successfully than if you devoted half the work to one type of institution and the other half to the other.

Pleasure in Language

At the opening of this chapter I said that literary language should give pleasure in itself as music does. Easy to say but a challenge to do.

To begin, keep in mind an essential point that I have made earlier: literary techniques such as style, tone, implication, and rhythm are not adornments.

They are not baubles that decorate a Christmas tree. They should be woven into the work so subtly that they do not stand out as devices.

If you use a metaphor or a simile, for example, make sure that it was selected to enhance our understanding of the abstraction, not merely for show like a diamond on a crown. If you use variations in sentence length to create a rhythmical effect, don't end every paragraph with a three-word zinger. That draws attention to technique and to you as author; in the process, it upstages the content of the work. A cardinal sin!

How do you learn what is effective and what isn't? Once again, by reading essays. A book such as this one can point out what to look for, but only through extensive reading of essays themselves can you absorb the subtleties of how to make use of these various techniques.

Literary nonfiction can be serious or comic, gripping or leisurely, deeply personal or somewhat detached; but to earn its status as "literary," it must be presented with language that is fresh and effective. The goal is not just clarity, it is artistic creativity as well.

7

ETHICAL QUESTIONS:

How Much Is Real?

*Names and identities of people. Tinkering with places. Liberties with
dialogue and thoughts. Omissions and additions. How to avoid
consolidations. The writer's commitment to truth.*

The border between literary nonfiction and fiction is poorly marked. Opinions
vary. Some nonfiction writers insist on using only known and verifiable facts
while others feel free to create dialogue and merge characters.

There is, however, general agreement on the principle I described in the
first chapter: when you write literary nonfiction, you adopt a fundamental
loyalty to events as they occurred, to places as they are in reality, and to people met or drawn from research. You are not writing from someone else's
point of view. You are not inventing details as fiction writers do. You are true
to the world as you see it.

Loyalty, however, is imprecise. These days when we crop unpopular family members from snapshots without a qualm, quote the thoughts of strangers
("He was thinking, 'Why should I do a favor for her?'"), and even tinker with
the weather when recounting how a vacation went, we are used to straying
from the truth.

It may be that you will want to adopt a policy of unqualified adherence to
the facts. Gay Talese, one of the most respected and prolific writers of literary
nonfiction, has lived by this policy. He even insists on using real names and will
not publish a work until he secures permission from those involved. He never
merges characters. And he is scrupulous about not using a subject's thoughts unless he is quoting a person's own memory of what went through his or her mind.

There is one real advantage to this uncompromising policy: you are never
uncertain about what is ethical and what is not. There are two disadvantages,
however. The first is that you may hurt the feelings of individuals you have
described. You may even risk bodily harm. The second is that you may feel
obliged to include peripheral details that clutter the account.

For these reasons, authors who are this uncompromising are rare. Many
reputable writers do allow themselves flexibility. Unfortunately, while some

adjustments are widely accepted, others stray so far from the facts that they turn work that is presented as nonfiction into what is really fiction. This is deceptive, a form of false reporting. Established journalists have been fired for making this error.

My hope is to present what has become a consensus. As a result, this chapter is an opinion piece, sorting out that which is accepted by most writers and publishers from that which is generally held to be unethical or even dishonest. These are judgment calls, but they are not trivial. If you are a journalist with a hazy notion of where the line falls, you may find yourself driving a cab.

Names and Identities of People

An absolutist's position is clear and straightforward: use people's actual names and ask them to sign an approval form. In a surprising number of cases, individuals are willing to do this. There is something flattering about being documented in print even if the treatment is not entirely kind.

There are a few risks, however. Occasionally subjects simply refuse to sign a waiver. Never mind that you spent days, perhaps weeks to interview, write, and revise. If this happens, you may be tempted to revise the section that apparently gave offense. But what has happened to your determination to be unrelentingly truthful? The other alternative is to shelve the work, hoping that the subject will change his or her mind at a later date.

A more subtle problem lies in the writing itself. You may find yourself pre-censoring yourself even in the first draft, softening your approach quite unconsciously with the hope of winning your subject's approval. It is a sad irony when a commitment to the unaltered truth results in an unconscious bending of your honest impressions.

Finally, you may have mixed feelings if the subject is a member of your family or a spouse. What is she or he going to say? There is a humorous but poignant illustration of this dilemma in the personal essay called "Snakebit" which appears on page 55.

Because of these problems, many writers take a slightly more liberal approach when dealing with people. We are used to seeing book-length works with the disclaimer, "Names have been altered to protect the innocent." In shorter works, this often takes the form of less formal phrases within the work such as "I'll call her Helen." This is unobtrusive yet clear. Readers accept it since privacy is a value we all hold dear.

Watch out, however. As soon as you use fictional names, you give up certain safeguards. When an absolutist goes back to the subject for a release, that individual may point out inaccuracies that can be corrected. Using fictional names obviates the need for a release, but it also opens the door to factual errors. More ominous, with no one looking over your shoulder, you may be tempted to delete certain important facts. You might be tempted to ignore the fact that the subject's husband was also in the room, possibly distorting her story without his saying a word. In reminiscence pieces, you may be lured into improving the weather, the view, or even—dare I suggest it?—your self-image.

That raises the question of fairness. We're all against "character assassination," at least in principle; but what about altering in subtle ways the moral character of a person through nonfiction writing?

Unfortunately, it is easy to do. Omissions are usually enough. Simply cut the responses that place the individual in a favorable light. What's left is technically accurate. And you may get away with it if you have given that person a pseudonym. But it is definitely unethical. It is deceitful because by presenting the piece as nonfiction you are implying a respect for the facts. This constitutes a promise to the reader, and you have broken that promise. It is just wrong.

The same is true when you bend the material the other way. Some minor omissions are understandable—a stray comment that is really out of character, for example. But consistently pruning your quotes to make your subject look good is not just cosmetic surgery, it is a deception.

True, you see this type of writing in print. Political biographies are notorious—both those that flatter a candidate and those designed to slash an opponent to ribbons. Corporate biographies dress up their subjects just as official portraits often do. And historical figures are given distorted portrayals by writers with an eye on sales. But keep in mind that these are essentially propaganda pieces. They are not literary nonfiction.

So far, we have been talking about interview pieces. The same sort of distortion, however, can appear in personal reminiscences. Quite often there is a tendency to dress up one's experiences, consciously or unconsciously. Minor adventures become slightly exaggerated; misadventures become disasters.

When this occurs without plan, don't chastise yourself. Most of us have an urge to dramatize our experiences in conversation, and rarely are we challenged. But conversation is fleeting and insubstantial. Literary nonfiction is neither. Even if you are just beginning, write as if what you commit to paper is substantial and potentially lasting. With this in mind, you will be able to be faithful to the people you write about—including yourself.

Tinkering with Places

Must you include every visual detail? Of course not. Every place, whether the simplest prairie town or Paris, is a great clutter of sights, sounds, and smells. It is up to you as writer to select those that will help the reader share your experience.

One of the most common errors made by beginners is to allow the reputation of a place to impose itself on what they have actually experienced. Suppose your subject is a place named, let's say, Windswept, Nebraska. We readers know what we *think* a place with a name like that should be like. But let's say you grew up there and enjoyed the camaraderie of classmates and the closeness of families. Perhaps back then you were unaware of the clichés about the alleged bleakness of the landscape and the boredom of small-town life. As you write, it will be important for you to ignore what others think and recall what you really felt about the place.

This is even more important when writing about travel to places familiar at least by reputation to most of your readers. Avoid the picture-postcard details. Describe aspects you actually saw, heard, and perhaps smelled, aspects that are unique in your experience. Good travel pieces reveal what the rest of us have *not* seen.

Liberties with Dialogue and Thoughts

The best rule here is negative: don't take liberties. Commercial writers have produced popular "biographies" that entertain the reader with entirely fictionalized dialogue and thoughts, but most of these are mass-market works composed with a greater concern for sales than for quality. Even when written with skill, they are works of fiction masquerading as biography.

There are a few exceptions. The one most frequently cited in this regard is Truman Capote's *In Cold Blood*. It is an in-depth study of two men who murder an entire family in a vain search for money. The events are described with chilling accuracy, but Capote also includes both dialogue and thoughts as if the work were fiction. It is a rare example of a hybrid form of literature sometimes described as *nonfiction fiction.*

This particular work is widely accepted as a distinguished literary accomplishment partly because the author spent not just hours but months of repeated interviewing. He came to know his subjects well. The fictional portions are based largely on what they said about their inner lives and on his close, personal knowledge of his subjects. The primary reason for its reputation as a literary achievement, however, is the quality of writing.

In Cold Blood is a work every serious writer should read, but it is not an ideal model for those who are new to literary nonfiction. Unless one is a highly accomplished writer and, in addition, willing to invest months or even years on a single effort, the fictional portion, the dialogue and thoughts, will seem artificially appliquéd onto the factual portion. It may also echo some poorly researched commercial works that attempt to imitate Capote's approach with more concern for notoriety and profit than literary excellence.

The use of dialogue and thoughts in literary nonfiction raises an important question: Why do we make such a point of distinguishing this genre from fiction? The answer is that readers approach each type of writing with a different set of assumptions. They assume that in a work of literary nonfiction the characters are based on real people, the places actually exist, the historical events did, in fact, happen. Readers are discovering aspects of our world directly, and unlike newspaper accounts, the view is presented with depth and with feeling. This gives pleasure and also provides insights.

With fiction, on the other hand, the reader enters a fantasy world, a dream. Even if the events, places, and characters are, as in some dreams, close to those in life, the act of reading is a removal from our waking world, an entrance into an as-if world. This generates a different sort of pleasure.

These two types of literary experience are fundamentally different. With some exceptions, mixing them becomes a deceit and adulterates the assets of each. The reader is left in doubt about whether the experience is a view of actual life or a trip into fantasy.

We as writers are obliged to distinguish the two approaches not because of rules or even because of traditions; we should respond to the expectations and responses of readers to two different types of literary experience.

Omissions and Additions

Most omissions are well justified. When we describe an experience orally, we know (or ought to know) that even our best friends won't keep listening forever. Nonstop talkers soon lose their audience. The same applies to literary nonfiction. In planning a new piece, we have to select what to include and what not to.

Suppose, for example, you are describing an actual three-day hike with four friends in which the final day was to be spent climbing a difficult mountain. On that ascent, however, you slipped, broke your ankle, and had to be carried back to where they could telephone for help. If your nonfiction description is to be relatively short, you might decide to start with that final day and to exclude the weeks you spent on crutches. This is the kind of compression that helps to establish the limits or boundaries of your essay.

There are, however, omissions that are less truthful. Suppose you decided to delete your four friends, leaving you stranded at 8,000 feet without a soul to help you. It may seem more dramatic, but it is no longer nonfiction. And if you submit it as such, you are being dishonest.

Judging what kinds of omissions are acceptable is not always easy. If in doubt, try to find a way to account for the missing detail in a phrase or two. If you don't want to give full descriptions of all four companions, for example, you can account for them and still place them in the background with a sentence like this: "The other two were new to me and I didn't really get to know them as well as I thought I would." In the same way, you can account for the passage of time with "The following day was uneventful."

The reality check is to imagine your piece being read by those who were there. Have you omitted some important detail that would prompt them to object? If not, your omissions are simply a matter of defining the scope and highlighting the theme you have in mind.

Additions, on the other hand, are always wrong. There is no gray area there. Jacking that mountain up from 8,000 feet to 20,000 to impress your readers is dishonest. Adding more days to the rescue operation, having helicopters join in the search, throwing in a blizzard for effect all violate your pledge to the reader that this actually happened. If you feel an overwhelming need to invent, switch the piece to fiction and invent with a free conscience.

How to Avoid Consolidations

Consolidations come in many forms, all tempting and all wrong. Like additions, they present a fictional invention in a work that promised no deceits.

Most consolidations occur in interviews. The views of several individuals are merged and presented as if they were expressed by a single person. This is tempting because it adds a sharp focus to the piece. But no matter how well intended the subterfuge is, that composite person is a fictional invention. He or she doesn't exist. Virtual characters don't count. Well-established journalists have lost their jobs for inventing characters in allegedly nonfiction work.

Consolidation can also be a temptation when describing a number of different experiences. Blending several episodes drawn from a summer job on a turkey farm, for example, and presenting them as if they all happened on one day may make good fiction, but it isn't nonfiction and shouldn't be presented as such.

Fortunately, there are several ways to avoid both types of consolidation without losing a sharp focus. If, for example, you have interviewed four children who were injured in a school-bus accident, make it clear that you spoke with all four and then concentrate on the one who was the most articulate. Just be careful not to attribute statements made by others to the one you have selected. Another tactic is to mention all four and then focus on two, highlighting either the similarities or the differences in their reactions.

Going back to the turkey-farm example, rather than consolidating several incidents and ascribing them to a single day, consider presenting a sequence, indicating which occurred on your first day, which after the first week, and which drove you to quit the job at the end of three weeks. Or you may have to make a selection, excluding some incidents and concentrating on one. Once again, don't bend the events to fit a fictitious account; rely instead on actual details that have impact because they are true to experience.

The Writer's Commitment to Truth

Ethical considerations are rarely simple and neat. Simply raising the issue may start you thinking about exceptions. The best approach, however, is to reaffirm the basic principle. In this case it is that unstated pledge you make to the reader when you write literary nonfiction: This is what happened; these characters, places, and these events are taken from life; these opinions are really mine.

There is your base. When in doubt, go back to this contract you have made with your reader.

To refresh your memory about the specifics, here are six suggestions:

1. *Names of people.* If you use actual names, be sure to ask the individuals to sign a simple release form. If you choose to use fictitious names, state somewhere (preferably within the text) that this is what you are doing.

2. *Places.* Identify them and use details drawn from memory or from documented sources. Make those details specific. Don't fake it.

3. *Dialogue and thoughts.* What you heard or what was reliably reported is fine. Don't fill in the blanks unless you are Truman Capote.

4. *Omissions.* Justified only if they don't alter the true nature of the subject.

5. *Additions.* No. Leave them to fiction writers.

6. *Consolidations.* No again. Never justified. A consolidation is an addition.

Every literary genre has its boundaries. At times they may seem limiting, but keep your eyes on the assets of whatever genre you select. In literary non-fiction, you are presenting the reader with real events and true personal feelings in a way that will remain memorable. If done right, this can be a significant gift.

8

ACTIVE READING:

How to Learn from Others

Active reading: analysis and evaluation. The pace of active reading. The environment where you read. Reading notes. Using case studies.

Starting with the next chapter, you will be applying the principles of literary fiction already covered to specific essays. The focus will shift to case studies.

In the long run, your development as a writer will depend in good measure on your ability to analyze and evaluate essays critically. This requires a special approach known as *active reading*. Acquiring this skill, the subject of this chapter, is an ongoing process.

Active Reading: Analysis and Evaluation

Passive reading is the type we engage in most of the time. Much of it is for pleasure. When we read novels or short stories not assigned for courses our response is similar to what it is when listening to music. We skip over dull sections and abandon the work if we are bored. Even when we are gathering information from a newspaper or a magazine, we skim quickly over what doesn't interest us. In both cases we focus on content, not style or tone.

Active reading, on the other hand, is both analytical and evaluative. It is the approach we use when we want to learn from other writers. As we read, we examine not just the content but the technique. From the very first paragraph we are concerned with the tone. Is it serious, humorous, snide, angry, contemplative? To what degree does the author reveal his or her feelings about the subject matter? What cues establish that tone?

As we move into the work, we look at how it is organized. If there are events, are they presented in a chronological order, or are there **flashbacks**? If different time periods are used, how does the author introduce them, and what cues indicate that they are concluded? If it is a contemplative work, how does the author move from one aspect to the next?

Active readers are also on the lookout for aspects of style. Is it straightforward, or are there **similes** and **metaphors**? Does it develop **symbolic** details? Are there **prose rhythms**?

When you complete that analysis, you enter the tricky area of evaluation. This is not just a matter of "I like it" or "They published *that?*" It requires setting standards about what is successful writing and then applying those standards. You may be reluctant to make value judgments, but you probably have strong feelings about what is successful in music, figure skating, and films, so don't be shy about literary nonfiction. Some aspects or sections of an essay may, in your view, work well; others may seem deficient. In examining them, you will be building your own sense of aesthetics. In addition, you will be asking yourself how you would have handled the topic differently.

Active reading means finishing work you don't find entertaining. This isn't as onerous as you might think; teachers do it regularly. You don't have to give grades, but you can learn from essays that strike you as unsuccessful. Ask yourself just where the fault lies. Is it the subject matter? If so, what conclusions can you draw about unpromising topics? Is it the length? If so, figure out where you would have cut. Is it boring? Perhaps dialogue or more vivid incidents would have added vitality. Or is the style monotonous? The fault may even be the author's reluctance to enter the work and provide his or her feelings about the subject matter. Does that tell you anything about your own work?

From time to time you will read a published essay that seems perfectly competent but insubstantial. You may wonder whether this is really a work that can be called literary or whether it is an entertainment piece, the kind you might read in a popular magazine and promptly forget. Here you are dealing with **theme**. The work may rely on a theme that is obvious or at least not thought-provoking. Stop and ask yourself just what kinds of themes are fresh enough and penetrating enough to broaden a reader's vision. This may help you to take a second look at some of your own work.

To be realistic, there are essays you won't finish. But make sure that it's not just because they don't entertain you. The only justification for quitting in the middle of an essay is that you are not learning anything new about the craft.

Close reading like this takes time, of course. Why bother? Because reading analytically is the way all writers learn. A textbook like this one starts the process by pointing out what to look for, but acquiring real ability in writing depends on extensive reading. This is as true for poetry and fiction as it is for literary nonfiction.

There is a parallel here with the long process involved in becoming an accomplished musician, a dancer, or a competitive athlete. If you want to become a good violinist, you listen to recordings; if you hope to appear on stage as a dancer, you watch performances and study the techniques of experts; and who has heard of any aspiring basketball player who doesn't bother to study NBA games? Whatever the field, we learn from the experts.

The Pace of Active Reading

We live in an age that admires speed. Advertisements assure us that we can lose weight, learn Spanish, or acquire "buns of steel" in just a few weeks. Speed reading courses abound. The Internet offers instant term papers and even hand-engraved diplomas in the time it takes to give them your credit-card number.

But the fact remains that excellence in any field takes time and commitment. The first step in acquiring skill in nonfiction writing is to slow your reading speed.

This may be hard. For years you have been urged to read fast, to grab the salient points in a history text or scientific paper, and to focus on the essentials. This is good advice if it is merely the content you are after. But if you want to find out what makes some writing pedestrian and some literary, and if you want to acquire the ability to write with effective style, you will have to downshift. Take the time to examine more than facts. Look closely at the techniques being used.

Stop at the end of the first page and ask yourself just what kind of writing this is. Does it appear to be personal experience or a biographical study? Are opinions being expressed, or is it likely to take the more leisurely and perhaps indirect approach of a reflective piece? Is the focus on a particular place, or is it primarily concerned with a person or historical event? How has the author defined the limits of his or her essay?

Even at this early stage you probably will be able to determine what kind of essay this will be. Will it focus on a place, on a particular person, on an opinion? And what about the style? Is it wordy or sparse; are there metaphors, or is the language straightforward? Have you had to look up unfamiliar words? And don't forget the tone. Ask yourself whether the author is personally involved in the subject matter. If so, how extensively? Or does the writing take a more objective approach, closer to journalism?

Why take the time to look for all these aspects when you have read only one page? There are two good reasons. First, it will help break the habit of reading just for entertainment. The pause will put you in an analytical mood. It will help encourage you to focus on those aspects that will help you develop your own skills.

Second, the predictions you make at the one-page mark will keep you alert during the rest of your reading. Is the author *really* as objective as you first thought, or does he or she surprise you with a strong but perhaps implied opinion later in the work? Does what you assumed was a travel article turn out to be a historical account? In fiction, your attention is held by the question of what will happen next; in literary nonfiction your concern should be focused on whether the writing is as effective as you had hoped.

The Environment Where You Read

Passive reading can be done anywhere and with any kind of distraction—on the floor, in a bus, at the dentist's office. Background music is no problem for most; some even leave the TV on.

Active reading is a different matter. It calls for a different environment. There is no one pattern that is best for all people, but it takes some testing to determine your particular needs.

Electronic dictionaries (not to be confused with spell checks) are an astonishingly valuable aid because they are so quick and easy to use. Those who have them are far more likely to check the definition of an unfamiliar word, an excellent way to build vocabulary. But electronic dictionaries do require that your reading areas be close to your computer.

Those who take reading notes in the margins of a book or a notebook usually prefer to sit at a table or chair. But there is nothing wrong with a couch or the floor for those who are, in both senses, so inclined.

Think twice, however, about allowing auditory distractions. Music, television, and, worst of all, conversations of others have been demonstrated to reduce both attention and retention. Some people are more easily distracted than others, so you will have to test your own particular needs. But the bottom line is this: if you use the same environment for active reading that you normally use for passive reading, you will find yourself sliding into the rapid pace and careless attention that you adopt when reading simply for entertainment.

Reading Notes

An extensive study has shown that those who take lecture notes retain more than those who have not taken notes *even when the note-takers have not been allowed to review what they have written.* The act of organizing what they are hearing has transformed passive listening to an active process.

The same is doubtless true of active reading. As your eyes move along each line of print, your mind is not just merrily skipping down the yellow-brick road. It has to assimilate the content, the manner of writing (style), the attitude of the author (tone), and make judgments about the quality (evaluation)—all this simultaneously. That's a remarkable achievement!

Reading notes in a notebook will help to sort out some of these aspects and record them for review. Even if you never refer to them, you prodded your mind into organizing a great variety of observations.

For some, marginal notes are more helpful. Assuming the book is yours and the margins are ample, they record what is significant. Underlining words and phrases also helps.

Watch out, however, for a common problem with marginal comments. Many become illegible. Especially late at night. Scrawled comments are often as mysterious as a doctor's prescription. Others are cryptic. Fragments like "style," "good point," or "!" do little but reduce the resale value of your book. Be realistic: your marginal notes are more valuable if they make sense in a week's time. They should have the capacity to refresh your memory.

Valuable as good marginal notes are, they can be overdone. They do soak up time. Investing too much time with them can become counterproductive. There are two shortcuts that many find are effective alternatives. The preferred approach is to wait until you are finished reading and then write a brief paragraph. It should cover in outline form the type of nonfiction, the central concern, and two or three phrases that describe distinctive aspects of style. This will take less than three minutes, and even if you don't look at it later the effort will help place the analysis in your memory. A quick review after three days will double the value of what you have written. Brief notes like this activate the memory the same way photos help to recall a scene.

A less effective but popular method is highlighting topic sentences and samples of effective phrasing. This takes less time than writing out a paragraph, and it does keep you thinking about the material as you read. But as you review the work, it is often difficult to determine why a sentence or phrase seemed important without rereading the entire work. Highlighting will not jog the memory as well as a brief commentary. If you do use it, be careful, too, not to highlight too much. An essay that ends up looking as if it had been printed on yellow paper is no more memorable than the original text.

Using Case Studies

In the chapters that follow you will be reading 14 essays. All the analysis about technique will be focused on them. These essays vary not only in subject matter but in complexity, style, and tone. A little more than half of them have been analyzed in ways that should help you to read with greater insight and, as a result, write with a greater range of options. The others have been designated as "For discussion." For each of those, I have provided a brief preface suggesting what you might look for as you read. These prefaces may also generate discussion topics. Essentially, however, the analysis of these works is left up to you.

The goal of the chapters in Part Two is to enable you to be an active, literarily critical reader on your own and through that ability to become a more effective writer. This approach to literary creativity echoes how writers have developed their abilities over the centuries, long before there were creative writing courses or texts like this one to speed the process.

We have seen how a majority of literary nonfiction works can be viewed as conforming to one of six basic types. These subdivisions have not been determined by some academy. They have evolved by tradition, just as types of poetry such as the elegy, the lyric, and the ballad developed in poetry. The process of literary evolution is ongoing.

Categories in literature make analysis easier, but they are never precise. As you read the essays in Part Two, you will discover that these six approaches often overlap. Be careful not to read any essay—whether included in this text or in a supplementary anthology—in isolation. Try to compare it with one that has a similar approach or concern. The more you read, the greater your stockpile of essays will be, and the easier it will be to make comparisons. The purpose of comparing two essays is not to grade them from A to F but to analyze the ways in which the approaches are similar and how they differ. If you maintain this critical stance, the essays themselves will become your teachers. They will suggest ways to make your own work fresh and insightful.

Part Two

9

PERSONAL EXPERIENCE:

Focus on Characterization

"Snakebit" by Connie Wieneke. Structure: using flashbacks. The theme be-hind the experience. Characterization through dialogue.

Snakebit

by Connie Wieneke

As I dial my mother's phone number, I skim the first page of my story. On the computer monitor, I mouth the sentences, liking the way they roll one into the next, confident and certain.

When I was 6 years old a rattlesnake bit me.

Ask my mother and she'll say this didn't happen.

But for years now she has tried to convince me that when I was younger and we were still living in Bakersfield, California, that I passionately loved the neighbor's Irish setter. When I visit her in Seattle, she drags out the photo album and points to the half-dozen scalloped-edged, black-and-white pictures of a girl and a dog in a back-yard. I don't trust those images: of a girl that could have been me—streaked with mud, being licked by this dog I do not remember.

The rattler, though, in a cemetery outside of Havre, Montana, materializes as two red marks on the skin above my ankle bone. All these years, proof that a rattle-snake bit me.

Before my mother picks up the phone, I make it through one screen of text. When I hear her voice long distance from Seattle, I work a light tone into the voice in my head before I speak. I tell her I've called to get some "facts" about the period we lived in northern Montana.

"Why do you want to know?" she says. From 500 miles away, I hear suspicion curdling her voice. I picture her on the couch: striped acrylic afghan—she made it herself and it looks it—wrapped around her legs, ash tray balanced on the couch arm, a filter cigarette inches from her mouth, and a cup with the world's weakest coffee clasped in her right hand. She is curled up on the couch, looking smaller than her 5 feet 7 inches, though the mannish cut of her coarse gray hair—she goes to a barber because it is cheap—and the determined line of her jaw speak to a bull-headed strength I know too well.

I tell her it's for a class assignment. One thousand words about childhood. "I'm just writing a story, Momma. Nothing earth-shaking." I scoot around in my chair in the small house I have rented for the school year in Missoula, repositioning myself so I can scan the computer screen better. "No skeletons will be revealed." I laugh and begin reading from the screen where I had left off before she said, "Hallstrom resident."

It was 1959. Another Montana recession. The summer between my first and second grades at Devlin Elementary School.

My father had just rented a 15-acre farm a little south of the Milk River. The property rolled away to this low spot beside the new Catholic cemetery and belonged to Bill Kimiele.

"Your father's old drinking buddy," my mother breaks in, and without waiting for me to say, "I know," she offers up more information than I need. "We were paying $50 a month rent. Part of the deal was we had to take care of Mr. Kimiele's horses."

"Yes, the horses were called Molly, Polly and Ginger," I say, proud that I know their names. "I remember riding Ginger once with Jimmy and Lyn."

"I don't remember that," she says. "Maybe you'd better let me hear what else you've written."

"This isn't supposed to be history," I remind her before I resume reading from the story.

My parents' makeshift tenant farm was bordered by the Kimieles' fields of winter wheat, an east-west dirt road and the cemetery between us and Highway 2.

"Don't forget Mr. McConnell's cows and corn," my mother interrupts. "You remember? He was on the other side. Mr. McConnell's cows were forever getting out and getting into the cemetery. One time I got a stick and I got about 30 feet up to this one cow. Oh, boy. When I saw how big it was . . . "

"I thought his name was McCoy," I say, certain I had shared this name with friends.

"That was a TV show," my mother says. "'The Real McCoys!'"

When she starts laughing like a female version of Walter Brennan, I feel embarrassed by my desire to keep the white lie of the McCoy name intact in the story. I breathe in and then continue reading.

Somehow they scraped together the money to buy a silver and blue Nashua trailer. Vintage 1955. Bedroom in the middle for my parents and another at the back to be shared by my brother, sister and me. Living room in front, the window looking south across an unpaved county road.

"Your father had to borrow the money from his brother," my mother says. "Uncle Johnny."

"It doesn't matter," I say. "That's not integral to my story."

"He didn't really want to do it. You know, your dad was in a lot of trouble as a teen-ager and your uncle could do no wrong."

"I like Uncle Johnny," I say.

"That's nice," my mother says. "I thought you'd want to know."

"OK," I say, hoping that will stop her.

"We paid $2,800 for that trailer," she says. "I still have the papers."

That figures, I think, knowing my mother keeps absolutely everything. For the proverbial rainy day, to prove her memory intact. My last trip home I made the mistake of trying to find a box of college textbooks stored in the attic. To get to the books, I first had to move hundreds of clear plastic juice jugs, the kind with orange caps; a box of advertising supplements from the Seattle Times; at least five boxes of half-gallon wine bottles, all green and with their caps screwed on tight; more boxes, these containing clean milk cartons which my mother told me later would eventually be used for freezing fish my stepfather would eventually catch, and one trash bag filled with foam packing material shaped like squashed figure-eights.

I never found the textbooks, which probably meant they had gone the way of my childhood dolls: to the Salvation Army. In her poorly lit attic, I saw her weighing my anthropology and history and dolls against the vast security and possibility of plastic and glass, the scales tipping in their favor. She had no use for my books and toys.

My parents set the trailer up on the farm, next to a well, three rundown outbuildings and a rust-colored boxcar with the Great Northern mountain goat insignia on both sides faded to little more than ghosts. Late afternoons, the cover of the well was perfect for watching sheet lightning. In that lightning, I imagined sheep and cows rushing across the horizon, followed by horses. And Indians. Always Indians. Everything galloping toward the West. Everything in such a hurry. The lightning so far to the north we never heard thunder.

"That's not right," my mother says. "It'd roll up on us and you kids would go screaming into the trailer."

"I liked the feeling," I say. "I can still feel those first drops on my face."

"They were big and usually full of dirt," my mother says.

"Well, I don't remember it that way," I say, and then ask her why she, a St. Louis city girl, and my father, who'd only done sheet metal and tended bar, decided to become farmers on the highline outside of Havre.

"We were on 'relief' at the time," she says. "You know, welfare? We got commodities, basics. You remember the powdered eggs and peanut butter, don't you? We'd get flour wrapped in brown paper and the oleo came in clear plastic. You kids used to fight over who was going to squeeze the yellow coloring into the oleo."

"I hated that margarine," I say.

"Well, it got us through," she says. "It was doodly-squat there for awhile, but that was the happiest time of my life." She pauses.

Before I ask her why, she starts telling me.

"Your father wouldn't let me take my medicine. He said the epilepsy was all in my head. The odd thing was during that year and a half we lived out there, I never had any seizures. Not one. I think it was just being on that farm.

She pauses. I don't think that's the whole story, but ask her what my father was doing at the time.

"Your dad was working for Great Northern as a switchman, but he was on call, they'd use him if they needed him which meant he wasn't working much. It was a hell of a time."

To make money, my parents decided to raise chickens in the boxcar and sell the eggs. They sold for 60 cents a dozen which was high.

"They were brown," my mother says, as if that explains the cost.

They started out with 200 chicks, which came boxed like doughnuts. One night they lost 150, because my mother forgot to turn on the heat lamps. The survivors became her exclusive property. She fed the chickens scratch in the pen they shared with the horses. She shot at hawks with an old .22 to protect them. And she chopped off their heads when we needed something to eat. Chicken-and-dumplings. Fried chicken with "smashed" potatoes as we called them. Chicken noodle soup.

"You make it sound like all we did was eat chicken," my mother says. Your father went hunting. We had elk. One time even bear."

"Yes, but I'm telling this story, Momma. I can still see those chickens running around, blood squirting all over the place."

"It wasn't that bad," she says.

The chickens don't have a lot to do with the rattlesnake biting me, but they were connected to our living in the middle of nowhere, our closest neighbor miles down the road.

"It was only a mile, but you kids never wanted to walk that far," my mother says.

I'm thinking if she keeps interrupting, I'll never finish this story and my phone bill's going to be outrageous.

"Momma, I'd like to talk about the cemetery, and the snake."

"Well, I thought you wanted to know."

"I do, but I only have so much time and the piece is only supposed to be a thousand words."

"That should be about right." She hurries on before I can speak to tell about visiting the Simpsons down the road. "One time you got ahead of your brother and sister and me. When we caught up, you'd found a dead skunk and were sticking your fingers into it."

"That's ridiculous," I say. "You're making that up."

"I wouldn't do that," she says. "I leave that for you."

"Let me finish this. Besides, I've heard all about the Simpsons. The outside of their house was covered with tar paper."

"It was more of a shack," she says.

"OK. I know I learned to ride the Simpsons' bicycle on their gravel road."

"That wasn't there," my mother says. "You're thinking of the Keller family. Red and Ruby. They were out on the highway and had pigs. . . ."

"Not now, Mother," I say.

"You didn't like it when they butchered those pigs. They. . . ."

"Mother, I've never seen a pig killed. OK? Can I go on with this?"

"Oh, yes, do," she says, all too perky. "I don't think their name was Simpson though."

Because we didn't have any close neighbors, my brother, sister and I entertained ourselves. When bored, we'd go to the Catholic cemetery. It was a new one, meaning nobody was buried there yet. Three statues had been erected and we loved to play on them. We had to avoid the "caretakers" working there who would chase us away, especially once they started laying the sod.

My mother can't help herself. She interrupts. "No, it was still covered with sagebrush. Mr. McConnell's cows liked to eat it. That's where they were always. . . ."

"Cemeteries have grass," I say.

"Well, this one didn't," my mother says. "It was too new."

I control my voice when I continue reading.

The hottest part of the summer settled over us, and we'd gone over to the cemetery again. We were playing on a statue of Christ with children sitting and standing around him. He was obviously telling a story because the children appeared to be in rapt attention staring.

"A parable, darling." My mother again. "He was giving them a parable. You remember what a parable is?"

"Yes."

"You should come to church with me next time. You'd like the. . . ."

"Sure. I'll think about it," I say, knowing I'll never step foot in St. Thomas'.

There were several other Jesus statues, all of them carved from white marble with red marble bases. I don't know if I'd decided to go home or what, but I stepped down into the weeds behind the statue and heard this sound. You don't have to hear that sound more than the first time to know what it is.

"What was it?" my mother says, like she's talking to a toddler. "A rattlesnake?"

"Mother."

"Just teasing, darling."

After touching the snake with the toe of my shoe, I jumped straight up and ran. When I reached the ditch separating our property from the cemetery, I stopped to look where the snake had bitten me.

"Oh, hon. You shouldn't tell people that rattler bit you. They might believe you."

"Well, it did."

"You'd be dead."

"Well, I'm not. Can I continue?"

"By all means. I'm enjoying this."

I was sure I was going to die and ran home, yelling "Momma, Momma, a snake bit me!" She asked where and I pointed to my bleeding ankle, which I could see swelling. But my mother wanted to know where the snake was. I pointed toward the cemetery. She grabbed the baseball bat she had once tried to throw at a chicken hawk.

"No, I didn't," my mother said. "Don't tell people that! I used the .22."

"But it's true. And you never hit a thing." I hear her taking a drag on her cigarette and decide to skip some parts.

By the time the cemetery caretakers arrived, the snake had crawled out of the weeds and was maneuvering the open ground of clods and stones. We were all running around. It was like a Laurel and Hardy movie on Saturday afternoon. Nobody knew what they were doing or why. Finally, one of the men used a long-handled hoe to chop the snake into three pieces.

"How can you remember that?" my mother says.

"What?"

"Three pieces."

"I was standing over one of the pieces, it moved and I jumped."

"Yes, that's right," she says. "I remember that. We all laughed."

"I don't remember it being all that funny," I say.

I showed everybody the two holes from the snakebite. "Look at the blood," I said, pointing to my ankle. "I've been bitten."

"They were just scratches from the sagebrush," my mother says. "You were always cutting yourself."

I could have died, but my mother wouldn't take me to the hospital.

"You were fine. You're making me sound like I wasn't a very good mother. Are you listening? Nobody'll believe that snake bit you."

"Look, why don't you write the story yourself."

"Maybe I should," she says.

My worst nightmare is that she will and it will get published. "Well, nobody'll print it," I say.

"No, darling, I wouldn't even try," she says. "I'll only send it to you. Keep going,"

"Well, that's about all there is."

"That's not much of an ending," she says.

"I'm still working on the last paragraph," I say.

"Well, we stayed there another year," she says, "until things weren't so compatible between Mr. Kimiele and your father. Even $50 was hard to come up with."

She continues without my prompting. "We must have been a hundred bucks behind. We had to move. B.B.'d had a litter in one of the sheds out back. The kittens were wild and we couldn't. . . ."

"That's another story, Momma," I interrupt, not wanting to remember, but her words force me to think of kittens left behind on so many other occasions. "B.B." was the last of a trio, a wild black we left on that farm when we moved down the road.

On my computer screen, I scroll quickly to the last paragraph.

"Dear, are you still there?"

"Yes" I say. "I was just thinking. What happened to the snake?"

"What do you mean?" she says.

"The pieces? Of the snake?"

"I don't know. We probably just left it there."

I start keying in a new sentence. . . .

I decided to bury the snake and crawled under the trailer with it. . . .

"How did you carry it?" she says.

. . . *in my pockets.*

"It was a big snake," she says.

"Mother, it's just a story. Have a sense of humor."

"The dog would have dug it up that same night," she says. "Look, you were too squeamish to pick up the snake. The magpies got it or we. . . .

"Momma, I've got to go."

She says she has a parish meeting to attend. "This has been nice," she adds. "Next time don't wait so long to call. I love you."

"Yes, me, too," I say, and hang up.

I read what I've written about the rattlesnake and one thing my mother said comes back. When I asked her about where they got the boxcar, instead of telling me, she said: "I used to go out to the boxcar with B.B. She'd never bother the chickens. I'd sit there with her in my lap and look out the window. I'd talk to the cat and cry. I couldn't talk to anybody else. You know how your father was."

I never imagined her doing that. Back then, I never knew how alone she felt. Back then, I couldn't have understood this woman forced to take comfort in one small black cat. Back then, I couldn't have taken her in my arms and explained away her tears.

I vow never again to go over a story with my mother, knowing all along that I will mail this one to her, knowing she will write immediately, inform me it wasn't an Irish setter in the backyard, but a chow, and that we never lived in Bakersfield, it was Santa Monica.

"I know," I'll have to say. "I changed a few things."

"You know what kind of people live in Bakersfield," she'll say.

"No, I don't," I'll say, "but I can imagine."

• • • •

Structure: Using Flashbacks

This is unmistakably a personal-experience account, and the base of the story is an unusually simple event. The author speaks to her mother on the telephone. (If this were fiction, we would refer to the **narrator** as a *persona*; but when a work is presented as autobiographical nonfiction, we are justified in assuming that the protagonist is actually the author.) This portion of the plot covers no more than about 20 minutes.

Much of this personal essay, however, is focused on events that occurred when the author was six. Well, *alleged* to have occurred. That's where the complications lie. Did the rattler really bite the author when she was six? Her mother insists it didn't. And there are other fuzzy details. Did the author really know an Irish setter as the mother insists? Even when shown a photograph, the author has no memory of such a dog. The photo actually looks unfamiliar to her. Then there is the farmer recalled by the mother as McConnell but by the narrator as McCoy. In this case, the daughter recognizes the error but is tempted to leave the name as McCoy in the piece she is writing, stepping over the line from nonfiction to fiction at least briefly.

The mother and daughter do agree on many of the events, however, and we come to see them in a loosely structured **flashback**. Unlike most flashbacks, it is not presented as a single scene with action and dialogue. The events are recalled in fragments that we piece together. Still, they do give us a picture of much that happened that day.

Notice that while the narrator wants to keep the conversation focused on the day they saw the rattler, the mother keeps recalling other memories. These are just incidental comments, not true flashbacks. For the daughter they are irritating interruptions as she tries to verify the facts about that day years ago, but for us reading the published essay they are important details that provide glimpses of her mother's personality and her life during hard economic times.

There is, incidentally, an interesting though subtle distinction between the daughter on the telephone and Connie Wieneke writing the essay: the daughter on the phone is simply irritated at her mother's interruptions, but Wieneke as author has decided to leave them in. Her author's sense tells her that they have a purpose. In that respect, the daughter in the essay is a **persona** such as we might expect in first-person fiction. The author of the essay has come to understand more about the significance of the experience than she did when talking with her mother. Still, the essay remains a nonfiction literary work because none of the events or dialogue have been altered.

What can we learn about writing from this work? First, it demonstrates how an extremely simple event can introduce a flashback that in some respects takes over the story. The essay is a model of how to develop a fragmented flashback. Second, it reveals how uncertainty about the past doesn't violate an essay's status as a nonfiction work as long as that uncertainty is clearly identified. In fact, the disagreements about what actually happened become an important part of the theme.

The Theme behind the Experience

In the chapter on the ethics of nonfiction I suggested that if names of characters are changed that fact should be clearly noted. Further, experiences must never be altered if the work is presented as nonfiction. Has Wieneke violated these guidelines?

Not at all. We can assume that the telephone conversation is based on an actual event. The fact that daughter and mother have quite different memories about an event that took place years ago is also true to experience. This difference in their memories actually introduces the theme. Memories about events and people, the author suggests, are unreliable.

But that alone is close to a truism. It is nothing new. This is why I suggest that the disagreements *introduce* the theme.

If you look closely at the essay, you will see a more insightful suggestion: our memories become distorted because of our emotional needs. This is revealed in both characters. The narrator is motivated to believe that she was actually bitten partly to get back at her mother. Look at the self-pitying way she describes the event in the paper she is writing: "I could have died, but my mother wouldn't take me to the hospital." Here is a young adult crying out for the love and attention she felt she missed as a child.

The mother's memory of those past events is also influenced by her emotional needs. She clearly doesn't want to be viewed as foolish. When her daughter writes that her mother tried to kill the rattler with "the baseball bat she had once tried to throw at a chicken hawk," she protests. "Don't tell people that! I used the .22." True or not, she is doing her best to look competent.

Even more specifically and more intensely, she doesn't want to be viewed as a neglectful mother. "You shouldn't tell people that rattler bit you. They might believe you."

It is not the bite that concerns her, it's the possible perception that she had been an uncaring mother.

The essay never reveals whose version is right. It is tempting to spend time arguing about what actually happened on the basis of what we have read, but determining the true events that afternoon is not the point of the essay. The primary theme asserts what every trial lawyer knows: our memories are not only inaccurate, they are often skewed by our emotional needs.

Notice, incidentally, that this theme is not handed to the reader as a concluding paragraph. In fact, it is not stated directly anywhere in the essay. Instead, it is implied through the action and dialogue. As readers we come to see the significance of the event through how people act and talk, just as we do in life. In this respect, personal-experience essays can be similar to fiction.

Characterization through Dialogue

While this essay is a fine example of how to develop a subtle theme, it is also a demonstration of how to reveal a character through dialogue. What you will probably recall a year from now is how vividly the mother and daughter were revealed in just a few pages. They will stay in your mind not because of direct analysis but because of what they say and how they interact.

Not all essays focus on character to this degree. As we will see in the next chapter, some excellent autobiographical works concentrate on theme. "Snakebit," however, is as concerned with introducing a vivid picture of two characters as many short stories are.

The primary focus is on the mother. Look closely at how we come to know her. She habitually interrupts, her mind veers off onto details that seem to have nothing to do with what is being discussed, she is bluntly assertive. And she is defensive about how competent she was as a young farm wife and a mother. Except for one brief paragraph of physical description, all this is revealed indirectly through what she says and how she says it on the phone. Although this is nonfiction, the essay adheres to the practice followed by most fiction writers: it reveals by what it shows; it almost never analyzes directly.

Dialogue is the primary means of revealing character, but there is one strikingly vivid paragraph that provides visual details.

> I picture her on the couch: striped acrylic afghan—she made it herself and it looks it—wrapped around her legs, ash tray balanced on the couch arm, a filter cigarette inches from her mouth, and a cup with the world's weakest coffee clasped in her right hand. She is curled up on the couch, looking smaller than her 5 feet 7 inches, though the mannish cut of her coarse gray hair . . . and the determined line of her jaw speak to a bull-headed strength I know too well.

Notice, however, that this is conjecture. The mother is not present. The author is not telling us how her mother actually looked. This is how the daughter imagines her mother. Once again, we have to wonder if the selection of details has been determined by the daughter's own personal feelings.

When you finished the essay, you probably agreed with the author when she characterized her mother as having a "bull-headed strength." But did you notice that to some degree the phrase describes the daughter as well? To the end she insists that she was actually bitten, that her mother was an incompetent parent. She refuses to revise the statement in the paper she is writing: "I could have died, but my mother wouldn't take me to the hospital." She even reads this out loud to her mother. And stubbornly she will go on calling the farmer McCoy even when she realizes that it is not his real name. The daughter and mother seem to be equal adversaries.

It would be a mistake, however, to classify this essay as a revenge memoir like those often written by the sons and daughters of celebrities. Toward the end of the essay we learn how the mother used to go out to the boxcar where they kept the chickens and sit with her cat and cry. Wieneke's response is truly compassionate:

> I never imagined her doing that. Back then, I never knew how alone she felt. Back then, I couldn't have understood this woman forced to take comfort in one small black cat. Back then, I couldn't have taken her in my arms and explained away her tears.

While the author's relationship with her mother is charged with disagreements and irritations punctuated with flashes of anger, it is also rooted in love. The simultaneous mix of these opposing emotions is **ambivalence**. Ambivalence is what differentiates simple characterization, both the unrelentingly nasty and unrealistically sweet, from fully rounded and convincing portraits.

10

PERSONAL EXPERIENCE CONTINUED:

Focus on Theme

"Jack-in-the-Pulpit" by Christopher Clausen. Using multiple flashbacks. A central symbol. When theme upstages characterization. An essay for discussion: "Catholics" by Gary Soto.

Jack-in-the-Pulpit*

by Christopher Clausen

A jack-in-the-pulpit, the forest flower that looks like a hooded cobra ready to strike, once frightened me so badly that it gave me nightmares for years. I was a very young child who had just fallen down the side of a mountain nearly to his death (I can't say *my* death, for it was a different person, a different me) when I discovered it staring at me as though it had contrived the fall to bring me within its power.

The experience was so long ago that the memory is really a memory of a memory. Now, when I see a jack-in-the-pulpit, I associate it not with fear but with my brother Peter, who wasn't yet born, though he was about to be.

"Because of its predominantly green color," says *Wildflowers in Color* by Arthur Stupka, "this plant is often overlooked in the rich woods where it normally grows. It is a common herb at low and middle altitudes where it flowers from April to June. The tube of the spathe, often colored or veined with purple, may be 1–3 in. deep. A showy cluster of glossy red fruit replaces the familiar 'Jack' by late summer or autumn." The spadix, or Jack, is sometimes also called the Preacher because, at least to the eye of whoever gave it the name, it resembles a man standing up beneath an elegant canopy to deliver a sermon.

*Slightly abridged with the author's permission.

My parents had left Washington to escape the heat. They liked to hike; they took me, their only child so far, to the Blue Ridge Mountains. Somewhere near Front Royal, Virginia, they rented a cottage. From there, they— and I, to the limit of my tiny powers—made hikes every day. It was the only sort of vacation they could afford. Besides, there was a world war on; other amusements were hard to find. How young they were! My father, recently returned from a perilous trip to Australia and assigned for the moment to the new Pentagon, had not yet turned 30. My mother, two years younger, was now six months pregnant. It was, I suppose, intended to be their last escape to the mountains before a second child made such trips more difficult.

Each generation has its own tastes in vacations. When my wife and I feel the need of escape, we go to the beach instead. Perhaps all the rainy camping trips of our childhoods had the effect of making us seek the heat rather than try to get away from it. Just as the sea itself represents eternity watching over the shores of an uncertain world, so for many people the dunes and their waving grasses— so different from the flora of mountains and forests—are the very symbol of summer. Renting a cabin in the Blue Ridge is not for us.

• • • •

When Peter got sick, we were not terribly worried. He was young and strong; his prognosis was excellent. The doctors were confident that chemotherapy would quickly solve the problem. So he told us all in a flurry of telephone calls, offering reassurance and at the same time seeking it, before he went into the hospital. He was anxious, of course, but not really frightened. He would not even have to stay in the hospital for long; he could go home between medications, even do some work, and be with his wife, Pat. They had a son now, Bill, who was three years old. The treatments lasted several months, but by the time they ended there was no further sign of the disease that had attacked Peter's lymphatic system.

We celebrated his recovery with a family reunion in Ithaca, New York, where our parents had first met each other and still had many friends. It was late summer, time for the vacation that no one had previously felt like taking.

• • • •

What I remember best from that trip, apart from conversations, is a tableau of Lake Cayuga at sunset on the last day. We had gone there for what proved to be a rather disorganized picnic with some cousins who lived in Ithaca. Some of us hiked up Taughannock Falls, a brave few swam in the frigid water of the lake, while others just sat around eating or drinking. There were enough small children to keep each other busy while the adults did the things that adults do on such occasions. It was, I suppose, a fairly typical family reunion picnic. Someone had brought a bright-red canvas kayak that would hold two people in a pinch, and various members of the party had taken turns, singly or in couples, at trying to make it move in a consistent direction across the lake. There seemed to be a trick to it that hardly anybody could master; after 20 minutes or so of going around in desultory circles, most people gave up and rejoined the rest of us at the two picnic tables we had moved together above the rocky shoreline. By now the sun was beginning to go down. The children were getting tired; the adults were finally ready to eat.

But Peter had figured out the kayak. Taking Bill with him, he had paddled it around a point on the lake where it briefly disappeared, and I wondered when it would reappear and from which direction. I wanted to take a picture before it got too dark. Soon I could see it coming back in a more or less straight line, its crimson sheen beginning to dull but still dramatic against the darkness of the lake. Bill was sitting in front, leaning against Peter's chest and wearing a bright orange life jacket. There was utter silence except for the low, monotonous lapping of the paddle in the black water. I could see Peter's silhouette towering above his small son and the kayak (it looked as though only magic could keep such a top-heavy shape from capsizing), wearing sunglasses against glare that was now fading to twilight and a cap to cover the hair that was only beginning to grow back, his bare arms now holding the double-ended paddle in perfect balance above the water as they glided back to shore.

II

On that long-ago afternoon (was it really morning?) in the Blue Ridge, my parents and I set out along what I imagine to have been (but what probably was not) the Appalachian Trail. It had been drizzling (or why should it be slippery?). The sun had come out and the path looked deceptively dry. The sun had not come out; consequently the path was hard to see. We were surrounded by pine trees, and the path was covered with needles. . . . All detailed memories of early childhood are suspect. Only sharp fragments survive here and there. I do know that my parents both wore old-fashioned, hightopped leather hiking boots, treasured and carefully maintained possessions from the pre-war world. What was I wearing? Above all, what sort of shoes? God only knows. I have no recollection of wearing anything.

What I do remember is the complete lack of a transition between two states of motion: between walking safely along the path with my parents, and rolling uncontrollably down the side of a chasm that had no bottom visible through the trees. I must have slipped on the edge of the path, but I can clearly remember not remembering having done so. The knowledge of utter helplessness overwhelmed me when I felt myself gaining speed, force, momentum, weight, all those concepts that I had not lived long enough to understand. Children are said to accept most of what happens to them, however odd, as normal, because they have so little experience to compare it with. In this case, the sensation was too rapid to be defined even in childhood terms as a situation requiring new reflexes; as a change in rules that had made no sense to start with; as a just punishment; as treachery on the part of a mysterious world.

What I remember is rolling sideways faster and faster down a precipice of pine needles, not being able to stop myself, grabbing at stones that only hurt my hands, screaming (I can remember my own voice but no one else's) until the breath was knocked out of me, and—and—inevitably running into a tree that caught me smack in the middle and stopped me instantly. Once again there was no transition between two drastically different states. One second I was falling toward the valley floor a thousand feet below. The next I was lying in the angle made by a tree growing out of the steep bank. Lying in the dark, dripping gloom of the forest, unable to speak or scream, in the instant before I realized what had happened, I saw growing just above the level of my face the jack-in-the-pulpit, an emblem of bottomless evil and terror in the world.

It was watching me. I could hear it laughing at my smallness and help-lessness, as it simultaneously decayed and exulted. It seemed not only mali-cious but very, very old. I thought it was going to swallow me up like a nightmare. There was no sky visible through the branches.

Heedless of the danger to herself and my unborn brother, my mother threw herself down the bank to where I lay pinned, apparently on the in-stinctive principle that a child in the hand . . . Or rather *not* in the hand, but alive, endangered, and now visibly kicking.

• • • •

The second time Peter got sick was much worse. He had gone for four years without a recurrence and seemed to be cured. Now it was a question of transplanting bone marrow, which involved weeks, perhaps months of isola-tion. Before that could be done, he would have to undergo radiation.

By this time he was deeply involved in writing a book about nuclear proliferation. During the long, frustrating wait for an opening in the schedule of the clinic where the transplant would be performed, he continued to work on the book and, as much as possible, kept going to his office. He was on crutches at this stage—the disease had affected his hip—and as a form of thera-peutic exercise he did a vast amount of swimming. When we visited a pool with him in the middle of a Cambridge heat wave, we found his upper body more powerfully developed than it had ever been before. From looking at him you could not have told that anything was wrong. After a few weeks he switched to a cane.

The transplant went fine. While he was in isolation, he worked on his book. The telephone in his room was always ringing, which pleased him. He recovered quickly and was allowed to go home ahead of schedule. Pat and Bill were jubilant. He no longer needed the cane. In a few months he was wel-comed back to his office and to Christ Church, where he was now a vestryman.

A little more than a year later the third time came—without warning like the first and second, and this time without hope. The doctors had done what they could, and it had not availed. The family began to arrive, not all at once, to make what it was now clear must be their farewells. So did friends from the Washington and California days, people from the church, Cambridge and Boston friends in great numbers. Peter received them all politely, but it was not the same as it had been twice before. By now he had withdrawn to a place where only two other people could approach.

In the hospital he would wait impatiently for Bill to get back from his Lit-tle League games so that they could play chess together. When he was alone, he worked on the last chapters of his book, which was nearly finished and under contract to a publisher. If he could not live to read the proofs, at least the manuscript would be ready for someone else.

• • • •

There is no need to turn a sad story into a sentimental one. After a few weeks in the hospital he was dead at the age of 46. On the day of the funeral, it was 97 degrees in Cambridge, and the eulogists at Christ Church joked ruefully about how much Peter would have loved such a day.

When it was all over, we came home. I limped through the rest of summer school, and three weeks later, after Pat and Bill had gone to Annisquam, we left for Rehoboth.

My brother's life had been risked for mine, in a manner of speaking, before it ever began. But that time we both came out of it safely. The tree had stopped my fall before I reached a fatal speed. Our parents half led, half pulled me up the slope to the trail, terrified but physically intact except for a few bruises. Children's bones are hard to break. In short order they assured themselves and me that I was in one piece, dried my tears. One of them rescued my cap and put it back on my head. My father carried me back to the car.

Although she never forgot it, our mother suffered no injury as a result of her leap down the mountainside. Pregnant women are also tough. Some three months later Peter was born healthy and undamaged. Our father continued working at the Pentagon until the end of the war; there were no more trips through submarine-infested seas. Eventually we acquired one, then two younger brothers. We kept going to the mountains throughout our childhood, though Peter and I much preferred the ocean. We grew up, married, set out on our own travels. He had a son who now, at nine years old, is an almost perfect likeness of his father at the same age.

So in the end my fall, a run-of-the-mill event in the life of a young family, caused no harm to anyone—not me, not Peter, least of all our parents, both of whom are happily still alive. What does a child, what does a parent know about the future? Irreparable harms would not come our way for 40 years. The only lasting consequence I can trace from the accident is that I could never again see a jack-in-the-pulpit without experiencing a shiver of revelation at the garish, mocking image of violence, the abyss of death lying patiently in wait for us just below the summer horizon.

• • • •

Using Multiple Flashbacks

There are several different time periods in this essay. Some are highlighted through **flashbacks**; others are merely filled in with exposition. For the casual reader, these different time periods intermesh as they do when we listen to a lengthy conversational reminiscence. Writers, however, must look more closely. These recurring flashbacks provide a good example of how one can create the illusion of a casual monologue while in fact developing a theme with considerable depth.

The essay begins with an episode in which the writer as a child nearly died while hiking with his parents. That opening scene includes some background about his parents' enjoyment of hiking. It also mentions, apparently casually, that his mother was six months pregnant. This is a good example of how one can introduce crucial details early in an essay without drawing attention to them. The author is careful not to say, "Pregnant with my younger brother who later became a major focus in my life and the major impetus of this essay." As in fiction, it is a mistake to introduce too much too soon.

The account does turn to his brother Peter. Notice that this is when they were young adults. It is later than the opening flashback but earlier than the time of the writing.

When Peter's illness is mentioned, it is downplayed just as it apparently was in life. "His prognosis was excellent" the doctors report, and we as readers are reassured as well. As we will see, this false optimism becomes an important part of the theme. That sense that the future is secure is reinforced by that memorable scene in which the author watches Peter and his son kayaking back in the twilight, "his bare arms now holding the double-ended paddle in perfect balance above the water as they glided back to shore." It is one of those special moments in which we feel that our lives are in balance and the future is secure.

This is the point at which a beginning writer might be tempted to start a paragraph with, "Little did we know that. . . ." Creative writing teachers come across that phrase with depressing regularity, and they must repeat the admonishment, "No! When the time comes, *show* what happens; don't spoil the development by predicting it." This advice applies to essays of personal experience just as it does to fiction.

The author then signals a major break in the time sequence with the Roman numeral II and returns to the day of the accident in his childhood. When we first read the essay, that shift from the calm scene on the lake to the trauma of falling may seem puzzling. What is the connection? Where is this essay going? But readers of sophisticated material must take much on faith, and we soon see the logic of this sequence.

The red flag goes up for the family and for the reader with this sentence: "The second time Peter got sick was much worse." And indeed in the relentless manner cancer often takes, "the third time came." Soon the author's younger brother was "dead at the age of 46."

In Chapter 8 I urged you not to read these essays in isolation. You will draw much more about alternative approaches if you compare each essay you read with others. The goal is not to rate them but to examine different strategies.

There is a significant difference between the use of flashbacks in this essay and the sequence in "Snakebit." In Wieneke's essay the flashbacks are clustered primarily on a single day on which a rattler did or did not actually bite the narrator. The **base time** is clearly defined as the telephone call. The essay moves back and forth between these two time periods.

In "Jack-in-the-Pulpit," on the other hand, the base time is not clearly defined. That is, there is no specific setting. The narrator is not seen as making a phone call or sitting on a porch, say, talking to an old friend. All we know is that the author is an adult older than 46 (his younger brother's age as at his death) recalling previous events.

As for the flashbacks, they occur at different times and in different places. The two dominant ones are the near-fatal fall and the peaceful scene at the lake watching Peter and his son paddling home as the sun sets, a scene in which life seems orderly and without threat. The order of the scenes is irregular, starting and closing with the traumatic childhood memory with Peter's stages of illness in the middle.

This irregularity runs the risk of losing impatient readers, but there are two compensating advantages. The first is a matter of **tone**. The presentation is conversational, like a raconteur calmly recalling how he survived a nearly fatal fall in his childhood and how his younger brother died prematurely. Had he presented the theme directly, we would have understood it intellectually without feeling its implications. After all, we are all capable of merely nodding when someone says, "Life is full of risks," passing the truism off with a shrug. A very personal account helps us to appreciate the full implications of the statement and feel its impact.

The second advantage is more subtle. We are not born with an awareness of how uncertain life is. Our understanding of just how subject our survival is to chance comes to us in small steps. We learn through our own experiences and those of others. This essay follows that same pattern. A series of apparently unconnected events in the essay echo how we slowly come to understand the random nature of chance in our lives. This is an unusual essay in that the organizational structure with all its apparent indirection becomes a symbol for the way we gradually discover the full implication of our own mortality. Only after going through these experiences with the author are we ready to share emotionally as well as intellectually what he describes at the end of the essay as that "shiver of revelation at the garish, mocking image of violence, the abyss of death lying patiently in wait for us just below the summer horizon."

A Central Symbol

Fully developed symbols are rare in literary nonfiction essays. Fewer still are central. There is a risk of making the work seem self-consciously "literary" in the worse sense—that is, trying to appear complex in implication and elegant and style.

If you are tempted to use a symbol, however, "Jack-in-the-Pulpit" is a fine model to study. There is nothing half-hearted in his use of that plant. It is highlighted in the title, it is introduced in the first sentence, and then it is described in detail in the third paragraph. It returns again at the end of the essay where its significance is vividly described in the concluding sentence. If this much attention were paid to a symbol in a shorter essay, it would seem like a flashing neon sign. But this essay is relatively long and meandering. Not until we pull the flower out of context and examine it closely does it seem so prominent.

First, a quick review of how a symbol works. It is a detail (usually a person, place, or thing) in any literary work that takes on a meaning far broader than it would normally. This certainly applies to the special use of the jack-in-the-pulpit blossom in this essay.

Initially, we know only two things about it. The blossom, so admired by many, once frightened the author "so badly that it gave me nightmares for years." In addition, we are told that as a child he found the flower "staring at me as though it had contrived the fall to bring me within its power."

In the third paragraph the author includes a factual description of the blossom for those of us who are flower-illiterates. He has, in a sense, planted a seed (to use a **metaphor** to describe a symbol) that lies dormant until the end of the essay.

There, in the very last sentence of the essay, we learn that the author still sees that flower as "the mocking image of violence" that lies "in wait for us." It is a recognition of random chance that we would prefer to ignore.

This is a private or unique symbol such as I described in Chapter 6 because we have never seen this lovely blossom used to represent such a disturbing notion. The object as described in this essay has come to stand for something much more than its normal meaning for the author and, through our reading, for us too.

Now we can return to the brief observation in his third paragraph that the blossom is also called the Preacher. It is easy to skip over that point on first reading, but as we look back (the advantage of rereading complex essays) we can see that for the author at least the blossom is also linked to those who preach about matters of life and death. In fact, if you consider the theme of this essay in isolation, it resembles a sermon. But if it had been presented that directly, we might have stopped reading. This essay shows how one can cloak a serious message and an important symbol with the deceptive guise of a casual monologue.

When Theme Upstages Characterization

"Snakebit" highlights characterization. There is a serious theme in that essay, but the character of the mother is even more memorable. In Clausen's essay, on the other hand, the flower and its association with the threat of unexpected death at any age is more likely to stay with you. His theme has upstaged characterization.

It would be foolish to start arguing about which approach is better. This is not a beauty contest. But when you look over the first draft of your own work, it is important to ask whether you are more concerned with the vividness of characterization or the significance of the theme. What was your original intent?

An Essay for Discussion

The essay that follows, "Catholics," by Gary Soto, is one of several works in this text that is reserved for discussion. The analysis has been left to you to encourage active reading. Here, however, are some initial questions to get you started.

Although this essay is essentially a reminiscence, it is also a short but vivid character sketch of the author as a boy. How would you describe him, and which details give you that impression? He and the nun share certain characteristics. What are they?

Like a character in a short story, young Gary reveals more about himself than he realizes. This is one of those cases where the author of the nonfiction essay creates a **persona** without inventing details that are not true to life. In what ways does the adult author probably disagree with himself as a boy?

There are some strong opinions implied in this essay. Some are held by the boy and others by the author as an adult. As you identify them, these opinions, examine which words or actions reveal them.

How would you describe the theme in one complete sentence?

Catholics

by Gary Soto

I was standing in the waste basket for fighting on the day we received a hunger flag for Biafra. Sister Marie, a tough nun who could throw a softball farther than most men, read a letter that spoke of the grief of that country, looking up now and then to measure our sympathy and to adjust her glasses that had slipped from her nose. She read the three-page letter, placed it on her desk, and walked over to the globe to point out Africa, a continent of constant despair. I craned my neck until, without realizing it, I had one foot out of the wastebasket. Sister Marie turned and stared me back into place, before she went on to lecture us about hunger.

"Hunger is a terrible, terrible thing," she began. "It robs the body of its vitality and the mind of its glory, which is God's."

Sister Marie cruised slowly up and down the rows, tapping a pencil in her palm and talking about death, hunger, and the blessed infants, which were God's, until the students hung their heads in fear or boredom. Then she brightened up.

"With hunger, heavier people would live longer—they have more fat, you see." She tapped her pencil, looked around the room, and pointed to Gloria Leal. "If we didn't have any food whatsoever, Gloria would probably live the longest." Hands folded neatly on her desk, Gloria forced a smile but didn't look around the room at the students who had turned to size her up.

Sister Marie walked up another row, still tapping her pencil and talking about hunger, when she pointed to me. "And Gary . . . well, he would be one of the first to die." Students turned in their chairs to look at me with their mouths open, and I was mad, not for being pointed out but because of that unfair lie. I could outlive the whole class, food or no food. Wasn't I one of the meanest kids in the entire school? Didn't I beat up Chuy Hernandez, a bigger kid? I shook my head in disbelief, and said "nah" under my breath.

Sister Marie glared at me, almost bitterly, as she told the class again that I would be the first one to die. She tapped her pencil as she walked slowly up to me. Scared, I looked away, first up to the ceiling and then to a fly that was walking around on the floor. But my head was snapped up when Sister Marie pushed my chin with her pencil. She puckered her mouth into a clot of lines and something vicious raged in her eyes, like she was getting ready to throw a softball. What it was I didn't know, but I feared that she was going to squeeze me from the waste basket and hurl me around the room. After a minute or so her face relaxed and she returned to the front of the class where she announced that for the coming three weeks we would collect money daily for Biafra.

"The pagan babies depend on our charitable hearts," she said. She looked around the room and returned to the globe where she again pointed out Africa. I craned my head and pleaded, "Let me see." She stared me back into place and then resumed talking about the fruits of the world, some of which were ours and some of which were not ours.

• • • •

11

BIOGRAPHICAL SKETCHES:

Light and Serious

"The Hip Plumber" by James D. Houston. Using humor to develop character. Implying themes in comic work. "My Father's Body" by Christopher Buckley. The challenge of writing about parents. Handling long time spans.

The Hip Plumber

by James D. Houston

The hip plumber is underneath my sink, squeezed in between the flung-wide cabinet doors, working with his wrench to unscrew the trap so he can unplug the drain.

"Sometimes," he says, "when I am up under here all by myself, in the shadows with the pipes and the smells, I think what the hell am I doing in a situation like this? And then I just relax and say to myself, It's okay. It's okay to be here. This is where I am supposed to be. If I wasn't *supposed* to be here, I wouldn't be here. You know what I mean? What I am saying is, I surrender to that place and that time, and then I am at peace with it, I become one with it. Hand me that flashlight now, so I can see what the hell is in here."

I hand him the flash and he peers around at the stuccoed underbelly of the sink, the chalky corrosion stains.

"I don't take any of this seriously," he says. "I mean, it has to be fun. I have to enjoy it. I go out on one of these big jobs, where some contractor calls me in to do the whole kitchen and bathroom, and these other guys are out there, the roofers, the sheetrock guys. They're glum. They're walking around doing what they do, but they can't wait for the day to end. And me? I'm singing, I'm smiling. They say, Hey, you don't have any right to smile, doing this kind of shitwork. In their view, see, anybody who smiles must not know what he's got himself into. They think something is wrong with me because I really do enjoy what I'm doing. But hey, it's all one, isn't it? Work is worship. That's what I tell them out there on the big construction jobs. I say, Work is worship. They just look at me."

Now he has the pipes loose, and he is feeding the snake-cable down into the long drain, a few inches at a time, feeding, cranking the spool-handle ferociously, then feeding a few more inches of cable.

"You see, I am just a puppet. This came to me nine years ago. I saw that what I had to do was surrender myself to . . . whatever you want to call it. God. Brahman. The Great Force. The Oversoul. You name it. I call it God. But you know what I mean. You surrender to it. You are a puppet, and it works through you. Each morning I wake up, and I think to myself, Okay, what is important. Feel good. That is the first thing. Then, share it. Share what you feel. And surrender to whatever comes your way. Look at this snake. You know what it's doing? It's flopping around down there at the bottom of your pipe where all the gunk has accumulated. There is nothing wrong with your drain pipe, by the way—although I might re-plumb this trap for you one of these days, if you're into that. You have about a ten-inch loop here, and all you need is four, otherwise you have water standing on both sides of ten inches, plus these two extra fittings you really don't need. Who installed this stuff anyhow?"

I tell him it came with the house. He inspects the loop, eyes wide in the half-dark. He shifts his position. He gives the handle another crank, with another smile, the fun-lover's grin, playful, a prankster.

"What I'm saying is, the drain pipe is innocent. The drain just does what it has to do, which is be a pipe for the water. And the water does what it has to do, which is swirl as it descends, so that over the years it coats the inside of the pipe with all the little pieces of stuff that come down out of the sink, and this makes a kind of doughnut inside the pipe, a doughnut with a hole through the middle that gets a little bit smaller year by year. The doughnut gets bigger, and the hole gets smaller and smaller and smaller, until it is down to a very fine point—which is just like meditation, you see. But then one day, bip, the little hole closes. The drain stops draining, and the snake goes down there and opens it up, like the kundalini snake of breakthrough perception! And whammo, a channel is cleared and the water is flowing again!"

• • • •

Using Humor to Develop Character

How should we react to this? Should we treat it like an anecdote delivered by a standup comic, or should we read it as a sample of literary nonfiction, a biographical sketch complete with characterization and sophisticated themes? The fact that it has been included in this volume should give you a hint. But where is the evidence?

True, on first reading it will strike most readers as just good fun. It's not often that we meet a plumber who not only pours forth his philosophy of life but uses his trade to illustrate his beliefs. That's what comedy writers call "the concept." It even has an echo of some Monty Python skits.

The author has kept himself out of the essay, a decision that further simplifies the work. The material is not presented the way it is in "Snakebit" as a somewhat antagonistic dialogue between two individuals. The essay, if that is what it is, comes very close to a monologue. This adds to the temptation to classify the work as lightweight entertainment.

If we take a second look, however, we can pick out aspects of both characterization and theme that give the work substance. If we stay nimble, we should be able to examine these without crushing the undeniable spirit of good fun on the surface.

What sort of guy is this? For one thing, he's not stupid. The beliefs he describes may not be mainstream, but they hang together. They are consistent. They also suggest a certain amount of reading. His philosophical outlook has a strong dose of Hindu fatalism filtered through the Zen movement that has considerable following in the United States, particularly in California. So he is not just spinning a clutter of ideas he invented. The piece is more than a skit from "Saturday Night Live."

He is also no hypocrite. He doesn't preach one set of ideals and live another. He has translated his beliefs into a life style as seen in this passage:

> This is where I am *supposed* to be. If I wasn't supposed to be here, I wouldn't be here.

This is not resignation. It gives him a sense of pleasure and an ability to enjoy each day:

> I go out on one of these big jobs . . . and these other guys are out there, the roofers, the sheetrock guys. They're glum. They're walking around doing what they do, but they can't wait for the day to end. And me? I'm singing, I'm smiling.

Some readers may feel that he could be justifying his life of doing what he himself has described as "shitwork." But the author has not provided a single hint that this might be so. On the basis of the essay, we have to assume that the plumber is truthful when he says, "I really do enjoy what I'm doing."

Interestingly, we would be more justified in arguing that his cheerful demeanor is a front if that were all we saw of him. There is something suspect in the merry individual who never admits to having occasional lapses. But in spite of the brevity of this piece, it does contain a brief reference to moments of doubt.

> Sometimes . . . when I am up under here all by myself, in the shadows with the pipes and the smells, I think what the hell am I doing in a situation like this?

Presumably, the author had a lot of dialogue from which to choose (the subject is, I'm told, still a plumber and still a cheerful philosopher), and the fact that Houston decided to include this admission of doubt suggests that he intends his readers to see the subject as a real person, not just a cardboard cutout on which to hang a comic anecdote.

Compare this sample of characterization with that in "Snakebit." The mother in that essay is comic in her irritating compulsion to interrupt, to insist on her own memories, to bring up topics unrelated to what is being discussed. But she, too, is presented finally as one with a serious side. The picture of her in the boxcar surrounded by chickens with the cat in her lap, crying with loneliness is poignant. It allows us to see another side of the mother.

"The Hip Plumber" is much shorter, but the technique of portraying a character by showing more than one side is similar. Both authors have been careful to provide information that gives some realistic depth to an otherwise comic character.

Implying Themes in Comic Work

The **themes** in this short and comic work are even more disguised than the characterization. But they are there. First, the essay raises questions about the notion, prevalent in our society, that there is a hierarchy of occupations. Manual labor is placed low on that scale, crafts like plumbing and carpentry are placed midway, and professions like the law and medicine are placed at the top. Is that, the essay asks, justified? If work is, as our plumber states, a form of worship, what happens to that hierarchy? We don't rank forms of worship. The prayers of migrant workers are not classified as inferior to those of heart surgeons. That's a major implication for a short, funny essay.

There is another theme implied in this character's observation that many of those in construction work are "glum . . . they can't wait for the day to end." Why is that? Is there something wrong with our society, or is the fault in our attitude? If all roofers viewed their occupation positively as the plumber does, wouldn't their lives be improved? Wouldn't ours as well?

Finally, not all readers will agree with his notion of passive acceptance of whatever life offers, but such a view is widely held by many religious individuals from a variety of faiths.

> I saw that what I had to do was surrender myself to . . . whatever you want to call it. God. Brahman. The Great Force. The Oversoul. You name it. I call it God.

We smile at this because the speaker is a plumber, but what if the speaker were a Hindu priest? Is the statement itself comic, or is there something slightly weird about the way we decide who to take seriously? One of our problems in reading a work like this is that we are not used to seeing serious idea embedded in a work that on first reading seems as unsubstantial as the monologue of a standup comic.

This essay shows how essays that appear to be pure comedy can present serious themes and reveal characters who have some substance. It is also a reminder that even light touches of comedy can be used to keep serious opinions from seeming heavy-handed.

The following essay, Christopher Buckley's "My Father's Body," is also a biographical sketch, but it is different in many ways. It is far longer, more detailed, and more serious than "The Hip Plumber." But there are some light touches too, mostly in the form of minor **ironies** in attitude and behavior. As you read it, consider aspects of tone and, most important, **ambivalence**.

• • • •

My Father's Body*

by Christopher Buckley

My father. Who knew about my father? I didn't. Ever. He was a man who kept his distance from everyone. After I was eight or nine, I don't remember him having any friends, no pals or couples coming over for dinner or to visit. I know my mother found him a cold fish most of their married life. At some point in my presence, they must have embraced, been affectionate, but if so, it happened infrequently enough that it left no mark on my consciousness; I have no memory of them ever touching.

The last time I touched him was in 1983. We shook hands. I was leaving Santa Barbara the next day to drive a U-Haul trailer with all my possessions to western Kentucky where I'd taken a job at a state university. He offered dinner at Arnoldi's, a family style Italian restaurant and one of the city's oldest, a chance to get together with my stepmother Nancy, a chance to say so long for a while. Although we had been living in the same town for the last three years, we had seen each other rarely. He was always working real estate, I was teaching, and, realistically, we did not have much to say. We had narrowed topics of conversation to cars, music, and a little sports—eliminating politics and his far Right agenda. Years had passed, the late '60s and '70s were gone for good, and an amiable truce existed, but there seemed no reason to visit too often and press our luck.

So, after ravioli and a modest Chianti, we walked out of Arnoldi's in the late summer of 1983. Stopping by the sandstone wall, under the red glow of neon spelling out the restaurant's name, he stuck out his hand, and, after hesitating a second, I shook it. He said something about driving safely, calling. I remember being surprised, standing there with my father's hand in mine, only able to say, "Sure," and "Thanks." He was not a big man, about five feet nine inches, average build, but I remember his hand feeling heavy, harder than it once was. I looked down, and it was the same hand I remembered from childhood—fingers short, the skin very white with freckles.

* Slightly abridged with the author's approval.

Although he never worked at anything but sales, his hand felt thick, like a gardener's or carpenter's. That was strange, especially because he always took care of his hands. Mornings when I was seven or eight, before school, I'd find my father at the dining room table with a nail file—the only man I've ever known who owned one, though I suspect "grooming" kits were common in the '40s and '50s. We'd be getting ready to leave, and he'd come out in his wing tips, camel hair sport coat, and knit tie, put his left hand on the table, spread his fingers wide, take the file in his right hand and round the nails into crescent moons, with smooth curving strokes, sanding his nails to just the right length. Then he'd stand there and hold his hand out away from him to admire it before he attended to the other.

When we had last shaken hands I couldn't say. For just a second, standing outside the restaurant in the dark, I thought perhaps he figured he might not see me for a while, so he made this unusual gesture—at once friendly, affectionate, and at the same time formal. This was demonstrative for him, but then it was only a handshake after all, the same business gesture he performed several times a day. After the initial shock of it, I dismissed the sentiment I had momentarily attributed to that handshake, and didn't worry much. After all, we were both going to be around awhile, so why worry?

I inherited that feeling from him, the feeling that I was going to live forever. He professed belief in the Catholic Church, its metaphysical structure, an afterlife, though he never attended mass. He believed mainly, I think, in himself, deeply and unconsciously so. Believed that there, in the rush of experience, haphazard as we all were in a physical world, his body would be a coefficient of his will: he was impervious, lucky, and would remain so if careful, reasonable.

Apart from that handshake, I remember touching my father only two times. Once when I must have been three or four years old, some Sunday morning out walking, we stopped on the courthouse or post office steps of some small town in one of the middle eastern states. I ran up the steps in my three-quarter gray coat, and he caught me in his arms. My smooth child's face rubbed against his day-old beard, that sanded texture marking the moment, the connection that, unknown to me at the time, would have to do for a long while.

On the other occasion, I was ten and threw a jacket I refused to wear at my mother; he pushed me up against the wall of the dining room, his left hand at my throat, telling me I should never act that way to my mother again. I was conscious enough at the time to realize this uncharacteristic outburst was about him filling in the prescribed offices of The Father, which he rarely did. My antics had backed him into the corner of role-playing, into making a show of strength. He was, I thought, more interested in asserting his view of conduct than in any offense to my mother, yet I realized my behavior was enough out of line that I'd best keep quiet and let it pass. A little more than a year later they divorced.

I think his affection was really kept in reserve for himself. His mother, though also not an emotionally demonstrative person, had made him the center of her attention and emotion to the exclusion of his father. The light, so far as he could see in his life, was always focused on him. He was a man who would comb and recomb his hair several times a day, a man with charge accounts at Silverwoods and closets of tailored Hart, Shaffner & Marx clothes—tweed, camel hair, and herringbone jackets—a closet full of Florsheim wing tips and tassel loafers, shirts from the laundry always pressed with stays inserted in the collars. You couldn't tell the bills were not paid by looking at him. I remember my mother wearing the same red cloth coat all my early years at school, remember having to wear through a pair of socks to prove the soles of my PF Flyers were shot. I knew this about him, if I knew little else.

He was, I suspect, an attractive man and had some way with women. Looking back into my child's mind and sense of things, it's so dark down many of those hallways, I can never be sure. But there seemed to be friction there even though parents try to keep it from children. Years later, my mother told me of one woman he was seeing on the side, a rich woman. My mother got hold of the woman and told her that if she wanted him, really wanted him, she could have him, but it was going to cost something for my mother and me to be taken care of. That ended that one.

My father did keep late hours though. When I was a child, and into the beginning of my teenage years, he worked at his radio station almost all the time and was rarely home in the evening, always with the excuse that he had to go back to work. It didn't take too long for my mother to figure out why. He was in fact seeing Nancy, the woman he hired as secretary, who was giving me piano lessons on the weekends in her home, the woman he would eventually marry and with whom he would spend the rest of his life. My mother hired a private detective, and that was the end of my piano lessons and the marriage.

More than ten years later, when I was home summers from graduate school and teaching tennis in city programs, I noticed that he was thinking about getting back into or maintaining some physical shape. He would take walks for two miles each evening. I don't know that he had any specific health warning then. It was vanity as much as anything, because he had started to expand a bit about the belt line. But he was serious about his health, had quit smoking cold turkey one day and never looked back. By the end of his life, he hadn't smoked for more than thirty years. He was always taking handfuls of very good vitamins and got me into the habit from my early twenties. He even took a series of shots supposed to clear the veins and arteries of cholesterol, and was taking a supplement developed by a heart surgeon for bypass patients to help repair arteries. He never said there was a problem, never saw a heart specialist. More than likely, he figured he was practicing prevention, determined to live and live and live.

He must have been in his late fifties when he started the hair transplants. Because I was away at college, then at graduate school, I saw him mainly during summers, and he must have gone through the processes largely between my visits home. One summer, however, I saw the means of it all—the mess of liquids and potions, the showercap-like apparatus, the dark pencil-dot plugs of hair healing into his scalp in the front of his head. He would spend most of the evening after supper in his bedroom with all that embarrassing paraphernalia on his head. This was the largest blow to his ego, the loss of hair. But a year or two later, all the treatments done, he had managed a head of white hair he could keep in place. He let the sides and back grow long and looked for all the world like a TV evangelist. For years at the end of his life, he had long, almost eccentric hair. This, I thought, was an ironic twist on vanity, a turnabout from the late '60s and '70s when I had long hair like most everyone, and for that he had denounced me to my stepbrothers and stepsister as crazy.

The last couple of years of his life he looked fine and so seemed to feel fine. He kept up his walks, had a room full of slacks, sport jackets, and suits, a large gold medallion and chain he wore outside his shirt and tie. He had two sports cars on lease, a nine-thousand-dollar Rolex on his wrist, and he worked every day selling big-ticket real estate. He wore glasses larger than Aristotle Onassis's, which probably cost as much. Except for the allergies that had always plagued him, he was doing fine. Seventy-one, and other than malaria in the war, never sick a day in his life. He would not think of life insurance, retirement and the like. What was the point if you were going to live forever?

Early one February, my stepbrother Alan called saying my father was seriously ill, in the hospital, and I should come. I flew out right away but was too late.

What was really too late was treatment. My father had what he thought were bad allergies and then the flu. He had gone several times to his allergist, who had not run tests but prescribed more medication. The day before Nancy took my father to the emergency room, the allergist took an X ray of his lungs and pronounced them clear; they were, in fact, badly infected with a strain of pneumonia that was getting the best of all his bodily functions. When he was sitting in front of the fire that evening in a sweater, his feet and hands were still so cold that Nancy took him to emergency. The doctors immediately found the pneumonia and started him on massive antibiotics; he remained conscious for two days. When I arrived, he was in a coma and on every life-support machine the hospital had. The doctor told us that my father had suffered "multiple organ collapse"—the heart had only been pumping at one-quarter capacity for days; hence the systems were shutting down.

He lay in a coma for over eight days. I could only visit his room for a few minutes each day, though I spent hours in the visitors' lounge staring out the window to where the pier and breakwater reached out into the sea and mist rose off the water and mixed with the light.

I could not go up and touch my father. Though I did at one point speak and say I was there, I could not take his hand. I was just overwhelmed, and felt badly for him, especially knowing he had no idea what had hit him. I could imagine the terror and sense of betrayal he must have felt as he sensed his life slipping out of his hands.

Nancy and I agreed: no funeral. It had nothing to do with anything we were invested in emotionally or spiritually. We chose cremation as the best thing to do on all counts, except perhaps what he might have wanted—the body preserved. But it made no sense to us, and, of course, he had never spoken of it.

I did agree to go see a spiritualist friend with Nancy—a medium, an old and somewhat famous man, an honest man. Whether you believe in a spiritual continuum or not, if you met George, you would say he is honest and believes in what he does.

George said through his guides that it had taken my father some time to realize he was not just having a dream, some time to "wake up" to the "other side." The first greeting George conveyed was that he, my father, Nancy's husband, sent us his . . . well, "good wishes, affection," George correctly adding that my father was not the sort of person who would say he sent his "love." There were just a few messages for Nancy, and his parting words were that in the spirit realm now, he was younger than his son, in a youthful version of his body, a body glowing in the life image of his late twenties. The message was calm, meant to reassure us, almost happy.

At that tenuous distance between worlds, between realms, that was the last thing I would hear.

• • • •

The Challenge of Writing about Parents

For many, writing a biographical sketch about one's parents is extremely difficult. Nevertheless, it is one of the most popular topics. If you are aware in advance of the problems you are apt to face, you should be able to work out solutions even before you start writing.

First, there are twin risks that are equally serious. On the one hand are biographical sketches that are unrelenting hostile or satiric. At the opposite extreme are those that are unrealistic in their adulation.

Hostile writing can be therapeutic. Psychoanalysts often recommend it. But such work is rarely literary in the good sense. The main problem is that the motive of the author becomes too obvious. What is politely called a "hidden agenda" becomes a strident theme. In addition, striking that same discordant note over and over becomes boring. You have to be unusually clever to repeat yourself so often without losing your reader.

If you find yourself sliding into this pattern, see if you can find a kind of positive detail. There is no law that requires you to give equal time for favorable aspects, but some balance is necessary if you hope to avoid creating a cardboard cutout such as is used for target practice.

Oddly, unalloyed praise suffers in the same way. At best, it becomes boring; at worst, it is like an overdose of sugar. Such writing is mandated at retirement dinners and is excusable at funerals, but that doesn't make it literary.

Must you write unkind things about those you love? Not unkind, no. But realistic, yes. It is not up to us to canonize our friends and relatives.

Buckley's essay about his father is an excellent example of how to deal honestly with someone one does not recall warmly. The negative aspects are presented without apology or, it would seem, exaggeration. The father is described as "a man who kept his distance from everyone," a man whose first wife found him "a cold fish," and one who "believed mainly . . . in himself, deeply and unconsciously so." We learn that he was unfaithful to his first wife and, later, leased two sports cars for his own pleasure while not bothering to buy life insurance.

A dark picture indeed. But the **tone** of the work is not one of rage. There is, understandably, disappointment, sadness, and touches of resentment, but not outright rage.

Imagine how much harsher the tone would have been if the author had chosen to close the essay abruptly with his father's death. Instead, Buckley has included those visits he made to the hospital when his father was in a coma. They are described in muted, melancholy phrasing:

> I could only visit his room for a few minutes each day, though I spent hours in the visitors' lounge staring out the window to where the pier and break-water reached out into the sea and mist rose off the water and mixed with the light.

Without making a point of it, he captures his mood through the details of the misty view from the window.

In addition, Buckley has included the attempt he and his stepmother made to establish contact with the father after the man's death. Predictably, even that failed to close the gap that had separated father and son over the years.

Buckley's handling of the tone illustrates an important aspect of literary nonfiction. While writers are obliged to remain faithful to events as they occurred, they are free to select or ignore particular details. This includes when to start the account and when to close it. Through selection, writers of literary nonfiction have almost as much control over the tone of their work as do writers of fiction.

This freedom to select or reject details from experience can, of course, be pushed to a point where it becomes unethical. As I pointed out in Chapter 7, if a reader is led to believe that a work is true to life, the inclusion of highly biased details is deceitful. In extreme cases, the work becomes fiction dishonestly presented as truth. Such biases can be negative (as in vitriolic political memoirs) or positive (as in "whitewashed" tributes). Fortunately this is not a problem for most conscientious writers. Such distortions are rarely made innocently.

The essential key for those who plan to write about parents or close relatives is to deal openly with their **ambivalent** feelings. I have touched on this before, but it is particularly important when dealing with those who are close. There are many types of ambivalence: admiration and disappointment, fondness and irritation, even genuine love and anger. As soon as writers are willing to share such emotions, they assure their readers that the work will be honest.

Handling Long Time Spans

Short story writers tend to maintain a short time span. **Plots** are easier to handle without the interruptions of jumps forward or backward in time. Literary nonfiction, on the other hand, more frequently covers a period of years or even decades. This may be due to the fact that the reader is already assured that the events are true to life. As a result, there is less need to create that you-are-there illusion.

You have now read three essays that cover periods of 30 or more years. If you compare these three, you will see that there are a variety of ways you can cover major spans of time and still maintain a sense of unity.

"Snakebit" is the only one that limits itself to just two time periods: the telephone call (**base time**) and the day of the alleged incident with the snake. No matter how often the mother introduces other details from slightly different periods, the essay returns to those two major scenes. The advantage of this approach is clarity. Readers are sure where they are without cues.

"Jack-in-the-Pulpit" is structurally more complex. Although it makes full use of that opening **flashback**, returning to it at the end, there are scenes from various time periods throughout the essay. What holds that essay together is the theme—the random nature of unexpected death—and the symbolic representation of that theme in the flower. Readers must maintain faith that those reminiscences from different periods will ultimately be pulled together in some way, and they are rewarded for that faith. It is an unusual approach, however, to depend on theme rather than a narrative sequence to provide unity.

Christopher Buckley uses a third approach to unify the various time periods described in "My Father's Body." It is closer to the pattern we are used to in fiction. He begins with the day he as a young adult left to take a job in a different state. He recalls that day as "The last time I touched him." Why then? Because the event highlighted the distance that characterized their relationship over the years.

Later he goes back to reveal a rare moment of affection when he was a child and, at 10, being punished. Essentially, however, he follows their relationship through the years, concluding with the father's death and the attempt to make contact after death through a spiritualist. That sequence is interrupted in a number of places with speculation, but the reader never loses that sense of forward motion.

If you plan to write a nonfiction work of personal experience or a biographical sketch, remember that length makes a difference. Both "Jack-in-the-Pulpit" and "My Father's Body" have been excerpted from somewhat longer versions with the kind permission of the authors. The length of those works allows for greater latitude in organization. If the work you are planning will be relatively short, don't confuse the reader or risk the sense of forward motion with a highly complex sequence of time periods.

12

BIOGRAPHICAL SKETCH FOR DISCUSSION:

"The Day after That" by Tzivia Gover

Discussion Topics

"The Day after That" is like "My Father's Body" in that it is an extended biographical sketch, but its **tone** is significantly different. When you have finished reading it, ask yourself just how the tone in each essay differs. In considering this, examine the relationship between author and subject in each case. Your analysis will be more precise and useful if you pick out specific wording or incidents that determine that tone.

If this were a newspaper article, the essay would be more objective. Writing literary nonfiction, however, has allowed the author to let some of her personal feelings about her subject to show through. Pick out some of the details that reveal those feelings without expressing them directly.

Next, define the theme of this essay in one complete sentence. Don't be content with a phrase; make it a full sentence with a subject and a verb. Your wording will not be the same as that of other readers since there is no one correct interpretation, but in any group there will be a consensus.

In defining the theme you will have to ask yourself whether the **focus** of this essay is on the central character, on aspects of teaching, or some larger concern.

Finally, examine the organization. Where does the essay start? If the opening is **base time**, pick out the flashbacks that occur later. How many are there? (Suggestion: examine the topic sentences at the beginnings of paragraphs.) What phrases introduce those flashbacks, and how does the author indicate that we have returned to base time?

Keep these questions in mind as you read the essay for the first time, but you will want to review them before you begin your second and more analytical reading.

The Day after That

by Tzivia Gover

By lunchtime, Daniel Judah Sklar has taught playwriting to four junior high school classes at the Emily Dickinson School on West 96th Street. That's part of his routine. So are the three flights of stairs he trudges up and down throughout the day. And so is the bulging tote bag, weighing down one shoulder, stuffed with student papers. Figuring there are 25 to 30 students in a class, this morning Daniel met with at least 100 students and each filled, say, two pages with writing. That means so far today, some 200 pages have been added to the collection that seems to splash over the sides of his bag. Daniel has been meeting with these students weekly for the past five months, so each student's writing folder may be filled with as many as 40 pages of work. This means that even by the most conservative calculation, Daniel is likely carrying more than 2,000 pieces of paper. Which is why in the other bag he carries a folded cart like the ones people use in airports for schlepping luggage. Daniel uses it to bring the papers to and from school. Under his arm Daniel is carrying a thick, pink South American wool sweater that he shed during one of his classes. He also holds a dark wood cane, which moves in sync with his right foot as he pulls himself up one more flight.

I first met Daniel in the fall of 1994 when I was employed for the year under the auspices of Teachers & Writers Collaborative, the organization that employs Daniel and some 64 other writers who fan out into 110 schools in New York City, Long Island and Connecticut. So I am familiar with the routine, its trials and compensations. This has been a particularly rough morning, Daniel admits over a tuna sandwich in the teachers' lounge between classes. Last night, tired after reading his way through most of his students' work, he decided to call it quits and set his alarm for 7 the next morning, when he would finish the last batch before school. But as soon as he woke, he realized he should have gotten up at 6. So he skipped breakfast to add even a few more minutes to the time he could use to read papers, write his comments, and make it to school close enough to on time. For the kids his effort means that someone listened to them, that when Daniel promised on the first day of classes in September that everything they wrote would be read and commented on, he meant it. Week after week, following through on this promise has a cumulative effect, Daniel says. This morning seventh- and eighth-grade students opened their construction-paper folders to see his notes scrawled on their papers, "Good work," or "That's a good start—where's the rest?" Even an "I know you can do better than this" means the promise was kept.

Today keeping to his word has meant that his sweater was lost and found once already, he has dropped his coat, his pen and his cane at least once each, and when he went to order his lunch in the deli across the street, he inadvertently asked the counterman for wheat bread on tuna, rather than the other way around.

This may or may not go down as one of those days Daniel calls "day-after-that" days, when it seems as though the good things will come tomorrow; days that are open spaces into which some seed of inspiration might invisibly slip or some root might silently shoot down to a deeper level.

Daniel still looks boyish, even at 53 and despite the gray that has overtaken his longish hair, and the arthritic hip and scoliosis of the spine which have him walking with a cane. His features are delicate, his voice soft. He is not much taller than the sixth-graders he will teach this afternoon. The boy in him is never far away when he is in front of a class. That may be one reason his students care about what he has to say, despite the fact that his is often the only white face in the classroom, that he doesn't know about the things that interest them outside—what Sega is, who Snoop Doggy Dogg is or how the Chicago Bulls are doing. He still remembers how it feels to be one of them. In particular he remembers what it feels like to be the one of them who is having the most difficult time. The year we met, Daniel visited a class of 11-year-olds who were so out of control he asked me to team-teach it with him. Actually, the class was slated to be one of the six I had been hired to teach. But soon it was clear that I would need help with this one.

Before walking into the vast, brick building on the Upper West Side that houses the first- through eighth-grade classrooms of the combined elementary and junior high school, my last experience inside a public school had been when I was fitted for a cap and gown 15 years before. On the front doors of the public school where I would teach poetry and creative writing two days a week, a red-and-black sign warned that all visitors were being watched. Inside, a surveillance camera stared down at me, and a hall monitor wearing a T-shirt emblazoned with the international "No" symbol circling a gun kept watch at the entrance. Uniformed guards asked me to sign in and out of school on my first half-dozen visits.

The classrooms were so crowded I could hardly navigate the aisles between desks. Teachers I worked with requested that I provide my own paper because their supplies were so low. A seventh-grade teacher baked muffins and sold them from her desk for a dollar apiece to raise money so Teachers & Writers could keep coming to the school. One boy I thought was ignoring me just didn't speak English. When these kids don't have their homework done, they don't say that the dog ate it. One boy said it was taken when he was mugged outside the projects where he lives, and I suspected he was telling the truth. A teacher polled several junior high classes and learned that 70 percent of the students had been personally touched by violence, muggings, rapes, shootings, murders. The father of a fourth-grader described the neighborhoods these children came from. "They have to step over drunks passed out on stoops and walk past drug dealers just to get to the subway or bus" he said. "What their teachers don't understand is that for these kids, just getting to the school is an accomplishment."

In the classroom where Daniel and I taught that year, kids were literally climbing over desks to have a swing at one another. I was prepared to be patient and understanding but not to be ignored as if I were a ghost—even by the kids who spoke English. Nor was I prepared to have 11-year-olds wrestle out of my hands the comic books or Game Boys I had confiscated. Even Daniel, despite more than a decade of experience, couldn't quiet the roar of yelling and name-calling. He tried all the tricks I had seen him work magic with in other classes. He called on the most bellicose students to be the first actors. He found traits to praise in every child. He promised respect for them in exchange for their respect of him. He bribed them with improvs, their favorite part of his visits. I even saw him get mad at the students. But when he did, his voice was pleading, not angry. Some days we convinced ourselves we had seen the slightest progress. I stuck with it, reluctantly at times, complaining to Daniel that I didn't know how we could teach kids about respect, one of his pet lessons, if they wouldn't show any for us. He'd listen to me with the same patience he used on them, and somehow I kept coming along. On the last day, a resigned Daniel said to them, "Well, I guess we didn't do what I'd hoped we could." Determined to salvage something from the semester, he even met with the students in small groups to talk about what had happened. That class, he told me, was one of the most difficult he had faced as a teacher.

The following year I met up with one of the more rambunctious members of that class, a boy named Jason. What did you think of that experience? I asked.

Jason was slouched back in a chair in his sixth-grade classroom. "It was good."

What about Daniel, what kind of a guy was he?

Jason's face lit up with a soft, easy grin. "He's cool," Jason said, elbow cocked over his low chair,

What was cool about Daniel?

"Don't you remember?" Jason's voice became urgent, as if my asking the question at all implied some painful gap in our impressions. "Last year he talked about imagination. And he asked us what's our one wish."

Later when I told Daniel this, he nearly sighed with relief.

"He remembered that?" he asked. It was a "day after that" he'd been hoping for.

When Daniel first used the expression "the day after that," I was confused. "You know," he said, "like in that song from 'Kiss of the Spider Woman.'"

I didn't know, so Daniel began to recount the plot of the Broadway show. The couch where he sat in the teachers' lounge was partially covered with a tapestry almost as worn as the upholstery it was trying to hide. An easy chair with a broken leg crouched in the corner. A few plants on cast-off tables did their best to liven up the place. Teachers filed in and out, getting a soda from the Coke machine or walking past us to use the faculty bathroom in the rear of the lounge.

Daniel summed up the tale of the two characters, one a flamboyant gay man, the other a reserved revolutionary, who share a prison cell in an unnamed South American country. "The gay man is always telling stories about himself and expressing himself. The other guy is kind of repressed, angry. You don't really know who he is. Then they have this incredible song, 'The Day After That.' And the revolutionary says, 'I grew up poor, and there was nothing. Then I was thrown in jail here, and you know, it may not be tomorrow— we may not make this revolution tomorrow. And it may not be the day after that. And it may not be the day after that. But it will be the day after that.' It's a wonderful song," Daniel said. "But it also is, you know, a way of living life."

Suddenly he was crying. Daniel's burst of tears sounded like wild laughter. The storm of emotion built and quickly passed. "That's what I'm doing," he said.

The summer he turned 21, Daniel got a job at an East Harlem settlement house that served poor Italian boys. "These kids were very tough. These were culture-of-poverty kids." Despite the difficulty of working with these young men—"They were a very old 17; I was a very young 21"—Daniel returned the next winter to work with them year round. The young men dueled with pool cues, wrote epithets on the felt cloth of the pool tables, and worse. During an argument, one of the boys knifed another in the belly. When the police asked Daniel who did it, he told them. The boys found out, and Daniel was labeled a rat. "They made my life miserable after that. When I refereed the basketball games, they threw pennies at my head. They threatened me."

In 1993 Daniel nearly gave up on teaching. Two years before, he had published a book, *Playmaking,* about his work, and in some ways he simply felt finished. Also the physical pain of teaching was becoming nearly unbearable. He took a sabbatical and lived for a few months in France. "I knew the sabbatical was over when I realized I really wanted to work with kids who were genuinely interested." He wanted to teach kids how to be autonomous. "How do you teach someone to take control of their own life? There are a lot of psychological and political aspects to all of that," he said.

His solution came in the form of a free Saturday afternoon workshop in addition to his regular classes. His students have dubbed it DRAMA PM. The title is an acronym for the names of the founding members. Daniel began his new endeavor under the auspices of Teachers & Writers, which paid the rent for the meeting space and the students' transportation to and from the class. Daniel teaches them how to write and produce plays. With these students the process is as important, if not more so, than the final product. Showing up on time is a big issue for these 13- to 19-year-olds. Learning respect is another. Arguments between group members over anything from tardiness to creative issues are central to this educational experience, Daniel says. "Talking about it leads to autonomy, to not being a victim. The reason people accept a drug culture and a lot of other things is they don't feel in control."

Finished with his sandwich, Daniel balls up the butcher paper it was wrapped in and throws it away. Now he's ready for the climb to the sixth-grade classroom where he will teach his last lesson of the day. The 27 students are divided into five groups, each working on its own script. One and a half weeks remain until their plays will be produced for members of the PTA in another classroom upstairs. Daniel does not stand at the front of the room, where the blackboard displays the notice "No Gum. No Walkmans." Instead he takes a relaxed stance, hands folded on top of his cane, along the side wall, which is made up of a row of closet doors. "Have you done your blocking?" he asks. He invites each group to report on its progress. His chin reaches slightly toward whichever student is speaking, as if he is doing all he can to bridge the physical distance between them.

"Our group is doing good," one boy stands to say. He is wearing an oversized sweatshirt with the words "New York" printed across the front. "We have everything down pat. But we don't really have the feeling thing yet."

"Maybe I can help you with that," Daniel says. The next report comes from a girl whose hair is a maze of cornrows. "This group is like a puzzle. We're all in pieces," she says. Daniel's face remains attentive but impassive. The girl continues. "James is moving away. We have to find a new person for his part. We need two other girls."

"So you're having casting problems." Daniel and the classroom teacher, who is sitting on one of the mismatched desks in the rear of the room, confer loudly about who can fill in for whom. "What are we going to do for sets?" Daniel then asks.

The teacher answers, "They say they want to use cardboard-and-paint sets, but no one has brought any in, so I guess we'll have imaginary scenery."

"That sounds okay," Daniel says, turning back to the students.

The kids let out a loud groan.

"Okay then, what do you want to do?" he asks.

One boy suggests using big rolls of paper. "We can paint on it, then just throw it down when we need sets."

"That sounds good. Good idea."

A flurry of alternative suggestions follows. Daniel says that if they bring in the materials for any of these proposals by next week, he will allow them. Otherwise, imaginary scenery will win out.

A few minutes later, one of the groups gets up to perform. There is a barely tolerable din of chairs scraping and desks dragging as the students clear a stage area. Daniel sways back and forth on his cane, waiting. One girl tries to ask him a question, but he can't hear her. "Whoa, folks," he calls out, stretching himself up a little taller. One hand floats up over his head, "Wait, not everyone's listening." In a moment it is so quiet that only the whine of a siren passing three stories below can be heard.

The play is slightly rambling. A boy in the role of someone's father is complaining about the white people he works for. "They don't like when black people touch their food," he says. In the next scene, he is shot during a street fight. His recovery is nearly complete by the end of the act, but he has amnesia and can't remember his daughter. His daughter, in turn, is distressed and contemplates running away from home. She turns to the audience. "What should I do, run away or stay home?"

"Stay home," someone calls, "you'll never find a family as nice as that." The girl stays, and in the next scene her father's memory returns, and all is well. But the play still isn't done. A romantic subplot still needs resolution.

During the performance Daniel gives only subtle clues as to whether he is amused, impressed or, much less often, perturbed. When a girl in a pink sweater and jeans jive-walks through her part as a madcap doctor, Daniel indulges in a smile. His mouth barely moves, but his eyes arch into down-turned crescents. He jots notes on a scrap of paper he leans against his wallet, with a pen he borrowed from a student.

"That was a good run-through," he says after the actors take their bows. "Do you know what I mean by run-through?" Daniel is always pausing to define words or ask his students if they've understood. No one is meant to feel left out.

Back in the lounge after class, Daniel says flat out what I've often thought about him: "I'm a good teacher." He says this without pride or fanfare. "I can sort of hear what a child is saying and give what they're asking for. Sometimes the kid is asking for someone to be really gentle with them, sometimes they're asking for someone to reach out, and sometimes they're asking to be kidded with."

In many ways Daniel has long been looking for the kind of instruction he offers his students. In fact he says he prefers the kind of schooling they are getting to the type he received in the '50s and '60s, when the focus was on acquiring information to prepare students for college. Most people his age probably look back on that era—before taxpayers' rights legislation such as California's Proposition 13 began squeezing public dollars from the schools—as the golden age of education. But Daniel dismisses it. "It didn't work for me," he says. For the students he teaches, he fears it would have been even worse.

At the Emily Dickinson School, 70 to 90 percent of the students are part of the free-lunch program—meaning they are officially poor. Roughly 60 percent of the students are Hispanic, 30 percent are black, and the remaining 10 percent are either white or Asian. What the students need more than college prep courses, their teachers are coming to realize, are skills that will prepare them for life in the world they face at the end of the school day. Kids come to school angry about what they have to cope with in the world. "You can't just be dispensing information when that's the cauldron underneath," Daniel says. "They're struggling here to deal with the reality of lives in the neighborhood." A curriculum including lessons on subjects like conflict resolution, and creative programs like Daniel's indicate the school is moving in the right direction, Daniel says. "Here they are very interested in what the kids are thinking and feeling. This is a very healthy school in that way." This is not to say, however, that he is content with the way public education is being dispensed. He calls education cutbacks "frightening" and the people who vote them in "bordering on diabolically evil."

Taking my cue from Daniel, who always asked his students about their dreams and wishes, I often asked my students what they wanted to do when they grew up. Most of the girls said they didn't know. The boys, nearly every one of them, said they wanted to play for the NBA. It's not surprising. Pumped-up basketball sneakers and anything with the Chicago Bulls insignia counts for fashion here. The Bulls logo is scribbled obsessively in the margins of kids' work and decorates the folders where they store their writing. When the boys say they want to play for the NBA, they are saying that ballplayers are the only men they've heard of who have gotten up and out in one, sparkling piece. The girls are still looking for a role model.

The way out for these kids, which Daniel is attempting to help them navigate, is *in.* Imagination is what he teaches. "If you really do work with the imagination, you're saying what's important is what you feel and what you think. You're saying you're valid, you're important."

It's difficult to commit to an ideal whose results aren't always visible. Some teachers complain, for example, that even after all this trying, the kids still get C minuses on their tests. Daniel admits freely that what he's doing may change no one's life but his own. Still, despite the criticisms he knows are cast against him, he's driven to try. A crease deepens above his nose, and his dark eyes grow darker as he leans forward to make a point. "There's always going to be someone who tells you, you are just doing this out of your guilty white conscience," he says. "There's a lot of name-calling. And guess what? Maybe all of that's true. But there's something else that's going on, too." He pauses as another teacher walks past. "You have to have faith that something else is happening."

Faith, Daniel says, is what keeps him going up and down these corridors and the flights of stairs, even when his body is wracked with pain. "You can't assume that you'll have immediate results. You can't assume you will have *any* results. I just believe in good faith. That's a really powerful force, and that's what I'm doing. And it doesn't matter if I'm not, quote, 'successful.' I'm just looking for a day after that."

• • • •

13

OPINIONS:

Direct and Indirect

Defining the "opinion piece." "The Coldness of E-Mail" by Destiny Ward. The direct approach. Blending argument with a personal touch. An essay for discussion: "Strong Stories" by Joseph Bruchac.

Defining the "Opinion Piece"

If you reexamine the essays you have read so far, you will discover several that, while not true opinion pieces, do present specific views. "Catholics," by Gary Soto, is on one level an entertaining reminiscence of what it was like to be a rebellious and enquiring student in a rather rigid school. But I assume you were able to pick out some of the author's opinions about schools like that, about some of the teachers, and about the attitudes some people have toward those who are less fortunate. Those views are implied through the action and the dialogue, not stated.

"The Hip Plumber" is packed with very clearly stated views, but the essay is essentially a biographical sketch. We know what the philosophical plumber believes, but the author never reveals his own reaction to those views. He is neither proposing the views of his plumber nor is he opposing them. Imagine how that entire essay would change if the author had started this way:

> My life has taken on meaning and direction thanks to a young man who teaches with the wisdom of a guru yet supports himself as a simple plumber.

Even if the rest of the essay were unchanged, we would read it as an opinion piece. In its original form, the views expressed are merely a way of getting to know the individual being described. They are a means to an end.

"The Day after That" presents strong views about the role of teachers, about school budgets, about the condition of public schools. As in "The Hip Plumber," these opinions are presented through what the subject says. Because the author treats her subject with such admiration, we assume she agrees with him, but these opinions are peripheral. The essay remains a biographical sketch.

A true opinion piece states or clearly implies a particular view. That's its primary purpose. It may be a personal preference such as admiring the work of F. Scott Fitzgerald more than that of Ernest Hemingway or an argument about why the reader should vote for a particular candidate, but the opinion of the writer dominates the work.

Most opinion pieces are direct and unmistakable. Frequently they state the author's view in an opening sentence, sometimes called a **topic sentence,** or at least make it clear in the first paragraph. But not always. The author of the essay you are about to read, "The Coldness of E-Mail," devotes the first six paragraphs to the pleasures of the handwritten letter. Still, her intent, announced in the title, is never in doubt.

A few essays of opinion present their case by implication rather than directly. This approach is illustrated by "Strong Stories," the second essay in this chapter.

One way to test whether an essay is truly an opinion piece is to write out what you feel the theme is in a complete sentence. The reason I stress a complete sentence is that a single word or even a phrase is too vague. If your theme starts with, "The writer prefers . . . " or "The writer believes . . . " or "The writer insists that . . . ," the work is an opinion piece.

Classifying an essay you have read is not as important as clarifying the intent of one you are writing. If you get into the habit of defining the theme of each essay as soon as you are through reading, you will find that you are much more likely to stay on course when writing your own.

The Coldness of E-Mail

by Destiny Ward

> *Loneliness is never more cruel than when it is felt in close proximity with someone who has ceased to communicate.*
>
> —GERMAINE GREER

I wrote a long letter today. I took out my dusty stationery box, which had been lost on the top shelf of my closet buried under a million and one other things I've been "meaning to get to" for years. I delicately removed my precious box from the cluttered shelf and sat down, planning to write a letter to an old friend I'd run into earlier that day.

Then while I was looking for a stamp, I came upon a bundle of letters, long forgotten at the bottom of the box. Nostalgia hit me like a freight train, and as I opened each letter, memories of the man (who was just a boy then) came rushing back.

I remembered warm afternoons in July, writing and reading these sacred letters. I remembered how I read each one over and over until the pages turned soft from being handled, how each word and sentence was pondered.

The ink and the handwriting were so familiar and comforting. Even now I can picture exactly where I was when I read each one of those letters for the first time.

My mind fills with images of a lake, the sunshine reflecting off the water, and me sitting on a warm wooden dock, legs folded under me, lost in the rhythm of his words.

After finishing the letters I am brought back to my closet floor, alone and cold. Those letters, the simple ink and paper, had evoked happy memories and images. I had forgotten the feelings associated with reading and writing letters.

With the purchase of my computer I grew accustomed to the convenience of e-mail and message boards. I guess I sort of lost touch with him because our only communication for over a year had been e-mail.

I found that I only wrote a few words and usually only after he'd written me. I didn't associate any particular emotions with reading his e-mails. Maybe it was because I didn't recognize anything that reminded me of him in those plain black and white messages. Or maybe it was because of my haste in reading his e-mails.

When I go on the computer I want to be on and off as soon as possible. As soon as I log out of my e-mail account, the letter is gone. There is nothing left to remind me that he has written because I almost never read an e-mail letter twice.

After having pondered my revelations in the closet, I feel immediate regret for ever having bought a computer. E-mail is so cold and impersonal compared to the act of holding a letter, seeing the words, and sometimes even catching a scene of the writer when you unfold the letter.

I wish people could go back to the sweet simplicity of the written word on paper. Much can be said for the benefit of it. Handwritten letters are personal and comforting.

There is so much more room for expression. When I write a letter I put little smiley faces in the O's, I sketch on the side, write little poems, and take the time to make a long beautiful message. I used to put dried flower petals in the envelopes and use colorful paper. You can't do that on the Internet.

I vowed to change my means of communication. So I wrote my letter today. I wrote a seven-page letter full of images and words and expression, which I hope will evoke memories, or at least create some.

I hope the recipient appreciates the things I've said, and I hope he finds meaning in my words as he's holding them in his hand. Then maybe, he too will be touched by the romanticism of letter-writing.

Maybe we should all return to this forgotten craft. Wouldn't it be nice to reach your hand into your mailbox, and instead of finding a phone bill, pull out a thick envelope?

It has your name written on the front, and inside is a letter from a friend, and when you open it, you find poetry, drawings and dried flower petals.

• • • •

The Direct Approach

True Opinion pieces are to some degree arguments. They may be direct as "The Coldness of E-Mail" is, or they may imply a position as the next essay in this chapter does, but they have to take a debatable position. Those editorials one occasionally reads lamenting the fact that too many people are killed on highways and that hard drugs lead to crime are not arguments. Since no one is likely to take an opposing view, they are truisms. They are not literary writing.

If you are about to write an opinion piece, think carefully about the opposing view. If you can't picture someone taking the other side, you probably don't have a topic worth developing.

Destiny Ward chose wisely with this piece. The popularity of e-mail is still fairly new and appears to be growing. Those messages are quick, cheap, and at least as reliable as snail mail. When older people deride it, readers are apt to assume they just hate anything modern. But when a high-school student like Ward defends the handwritten letter, readers listen.

Ward has taken the direct approach. That is, we know from the title just what her position is going to be. But there are many ways to be direct. One is to define both sides of the argument at the outset and then to keep alternating with the advantages of one approach and the disadvantages of the other throughout the article. This echoes an approach often used in debate. It allows the writer to pummel the opposition repeatedly. The pattern lends itself to political arguments in which one tries to be as assertive as possible.

Ward's topic, however, is gentler. She hopes to persuade, but it would be a mistake for her to be strident. She's not running for Congress. Not yet. If you look at her organization carefully, you will see that she has divided the essay into thirds. She begins with a personal experience, preparing to write a letter. It's clear that she hasn't done so for some time. This is followed not with the pleasure of writing but reading what others have written to her.

Not until the seventh full paragraph does she raise the C word, "computer." This introduces the second of her three sections, her dislike of e-mail. Like a good debater, she lists very specific disadvantages: the electronic message tends to be brief, utilitarian; it lacks the personal quality of handwriting; it encourages the recipient to log out as soon as possible; and one rarely reads the messages a second time. Listing her points makes them seem like an outline for a debate paper, but she is careful to maintain an informal, conversational tone.

In the final third of her short essay she returns to the pleasures of writing by hand. It is here that she makes her pitch: "Maybe we should all return to this forgotten craft."

Blending Argument with a Personal Touch

The great majority of argumentative writing is not what we are calling literary nonfiction. Legal briefs, most editorials (even those with a significant point), political position papers, news items, even most letters to the editor are all forms of utilitarian writing. They may be logical, clearly expressed, and well supported with evidence, but they are not literary. As I pointed out in Chapter 1, they lack two characteristics: a special concern for language and a personal involvement on the part of the writer. Ward's piece is, like all the essays included in this textbook, written with a sensitivity for language and a personal touch.

Notice that she starts out not with an abstract assertion but a personal experience: that very day she wrote a long letter. Our curiosity is raised right away by the fact that her stationery box is "dusty." It was "lost on the top shelf." She "delicately" retrieves her "precious box."

She then turns to memories of reading letters from an old friend. The details are carefully selected.

> I remembered warm afternoons in July, writing and reading these sacred letters. I remembered how I read each one over and over until the pages turned soft from being handled, how each word and sentence was pondered.

Now it may be that she also read those letters on a cold and dreary winter evening, but it is her privilege as a writer to select which memories to record. Those "warm afternoons in July" set the mood for us. She then tells us that she read them "over and over until the pages turned soft from being handled." The phrasing has overtones of warm affection.

When she has finished reading those letters from the past she is "brought back to my closet floor, alone and cold." The mood has changed, and in the next paragraph she tells us about her computer. She regrets having bought it and blames it for the fact that her regular exchange of communication faded away. It may be unfair to blame the computer for the termination of that relationship, but that was the sequence of events and she makes use of it.

Returning to the pleasure of handwritten letters, she gives specific examples of what you can do with mailed letters—the dried flower petals in the envelopes, the colored paper, the sketches in the margins and little poems.

This is not a hard-hitting argument. The topic is light. But it is a genuine belief, and there are many who would argue the other side. Hers is a personal invitation to take her position.

An Essay for Discussion

The next essay, "Strong Stories," by the Native American Joseph Bruchac, is for your analysis and discussion. You will find that the author presents his primary point fairly directly in the concluding paragraph, but he also presents a number of strongly felt opinions indirectly throughout the essay. If you list his various convictions and examine whether they are presented directly or implied, you will learn a good deal about how to weave a number of opinions into a single essay.

Also take a look at how the tone of this essay shifts from gentle reflection at the beginning to flashes of bitter resentment. Where does this occur? How is it handled? With these aspects in mind, take a close look at how he uses the title of this essay. How does it apply to his own approach to literary nonfiction?

Strong Stories

by Joseph Bruchac

When people ask me what led me to become a writer and storyteller, I always tell them that it was due in large part to the influence of my maternal grand-parents who raised me. And, I add, my lifelong interest in my Native American heritage stems from my dark-skinned Abenaki grandfather, Jesse Bowman. My grandmother kept our house filled with books. However, as far as I know, Grampa Jesse never read a one of them. He could barely read a newspaper. His formal schooling ended in fourth grade when he jumped out a schoolhouse window after having been called a "dirty Indian" one too many times. Yet it is his voice that I often hear when I begin to tell a story and I feel his gentle encouraging presence with me as I start to write. Time and again, I have seen my grandfather's face in the faces of Native elders who have been my teachers and I have heard echoes of his slow, storytelling cadence and gentle humor in their voices.

My grandfather never raised his hand to me or raised his voice in anger at me when I was a child. I will never forget what my grandfather told me about his own upbringing. "My father never hit me," he said, "no matter what I done. He'd just talk to me, tell me a story." Then he chuckled. "There was times I think I would of rather had him hit me. Them stories was strong."

Years later, when I was in graduate school at Syracuse University, I would drive the Harley motorcycle that was my main means of transportation out to the Onondaga Reservation—on whose land the city of Syracuse had been built. There, as I sat in the house of my Clan Mother friend Dewasentah, I would learn that child-rearing without abuse, child-rearing through the telling of stories, had always been the norm for the Iroquois people, as well. Beating and harsh words can twist the spirit of a child. A story stays in a child's heart and helps that child grow up straight and strong. The more I traveled and listened, the clearer it became to me that throughout Native North America the rule was "Spare the rod and tell the story."

Strong stories. That is one of the things which most Native American authors of this last quarter century have in common. Whether they are poets such as Simon Ortiz and Mary TallMountain, Ray Young Bear and Joy Harjo or prose writers such as Louis Owens and Linda Hogan, N. Scott Momaday and Elizabeth Cook-Lynn, they tell strong stories. More than one Native author has told me how important it was to them to hear the stories when they were young, how those stories have remained with them. Simon Ortiz's father was well known as a storyteller at Acoma Pueblo. Simon once told me with pride how people used to refer to him as "the storyteller's son." It is no accident that an audio tape of N. Scott Momaday reading his own work was titled *Storyteller* or that *Storyteller* is the name of one of Leslie Silko's books.

As a writer who is also a professional storyteller, I have learned that the best stories—whether they are written down or carried on our breath—always serve at least two purposes. First they are interesting and entertaining. That way they will be heard. Secondly, they carry teachings which are morally and practically useful. Thus they teach lessons. No matter how well-meaning it may be, a dull story will either be ignored or forgotten. George Bernard Shaw, the British writer, learned that in his career as a playwright after discovering his earlier works, though earnest, were not being heard. The majority of Native American writers either grew up with that understanding or, like myself, rediscovered it as adults when they began to write seriously.

In the late 1800's, the American government embarked upon a campaign which was designed "to kill the Indian and save the man." Coercive assimilation was United States Indian Policy from 1887 to 1934. Native culture had to be eradicated to make the Indians properly American. Literacy was an important part of that campaign as Native children were taken from their families and sent to Indian schools. There their own clothing would be taken away and they would be put into military uniforms. Their hair would be cut short and they would be forbidden to speak Native languages. If they disobeyed they would be brutally beaten. Many of those children died of infectious diseases or committed suicide.

At Onondaga many of the children were taken to the Thomas Indian Boarding School. "It was awful," Dewasentah said to me, remembering those days when the truck would come to take the children away. "The parents had been told it was best for their children, so they would have them ready. But the children would cry and scream for their parents as they dragged them away. I can still hear them crying."

The irony of that government effort was that it developed a deep interest in books among the graduates of those schools. Some of those who came back believed what the government had taught them about their old ways being wrong. But among some the opposite was true. Many of the graduates of such Indian Schools as Carlisle in Pennsylvania became strong advocates for Native culture and Native rights. Instead of forgetting the old stories, they added in a love of written literature. I cannot tell you how often I have entered the homes of Native elders who were boarding school survivors and found the walls lined, like Dewasentah's, with books—most of them about Indians. It was not an uncritical love of books, I might add, for those elders were usually quick to point out to me the books in their collections which (invariably written by non-Indian Indian experts) contained lies about their people.

When I went to West Africa as a volunteer teacher in the 1960's I became friends with Chinua Achebe, a well-known African novelist. Chinua told me straightforwardly that one of the major reasons he became a writer was a British novel called *Mr. Johnson,* which portrayed Achebe's Igbo people as ignorant, dirty, and superstitious. Achebe, who had grown up in a spiritually rich storytelling tradition, wanted to tell a different story and did so in a magnificent first novel called *Things Fall Apart.*

That, of course, is the wonderful irony about literacy. If a supposedly superior culture forces literacy upon Native cultures, that "superior" culture then finds—to the dismay of the missionaries—that being able to read means being able to read not just the approved books, but also those which tell the other side of the story. Being able to write means the Natives will find ways to express the values of their original cultures in that new medium and that new language.

And so it is today. The works of the Native writers of the last three decades continue to tell those strong old stories, stories of spiritual survival, in poems and stories, in novels and essays and plays written in large part in English. The children and grandchildren of those who were taken from their homes by force and taught to have contempt for their tribal cultures today look back to the oral tradition, are inspired by it, and then continue the circle of stories, continue it through their writing.

14

REFLECTIONS:

Discursive Writing with a Purpose

The hidden order in reflective essays. "Stone's Throw" by Jackson Jodie Daviss. Marginal notes that help. Wordplay: metaphors, puns, symbolic stones. An essay for discussion: "Total Laryngitis" by Trinie Dalton.

Hidden Order

We think of reflective pieces as thoughtful, contemplative, meditative. They tend to be less structured than other types of literary nonfiction. They may appear to meander. You might think that reflective work would be easier to write.

Not so. If anything, the **reflective essay** is more difficult. The problem is maintaining a hidden structure. When you are working with personal experience, you usually have a **plot** to guide you. In "Snakebit," for example, the telephone call itself provides forward movement, and the repeated flashbacks to the day in the author's childhood also progress in time, moving from the discovery of the snake to its death and dismemberment. There are plenty of detours along the way, but the reader always knows where the work is going.

"Jack-in-the-Pulpit" is more fragmentary, but soon it is clear that there is a narrative sequence following the life, the illness, and the tragically early death of the author's brother Peter. The chronological use of the passing years, broken only by flashbacks, is similar to the organization used in Christopher Buckley's "My Father's Body."

Opinion pieces are often personal, but as we have seen they are frequently organized like arguments. The progression of events that often provides structure in personal-experience pieces and some biographical sketches is replaced with a progression of ideas.

Reflective pieces are less likely to have a narrative thread, and if there is a logical sequence it tends to be vague or hidden. Furthermore, the tone is often deceptively informal, like a conversational monologue.

In some ways, reflective essays are closer to poems. Instead of moving event by event they often progress from **image** to image. One visual impression suggests another. The reader must take on faith that there is indeed some kind of thematic development.

This much freedom is a challenge. An essay that is too **abstract** may, like a balloon cut loose, lose all sense of direction. Abstractions like *life, immortality,* and *art* are hard to deal with unless attached to something we can see—like a rock.

Moving from the unmistakable organization of research papers such as one writes in school to the apparent freedom of a reflective piece is for some like shifting from the structure of metered poetry to free verse. With freedom, though, comes the responsibility to find some other way to give shape to the work.

One approach is to tie your reflections to a personal experience that will provide a sequence the reader can hold on to. It doesn't have to be a dominant part of the work. Just an occasional reference can give direction. Driving in a rainstorm, for example, or walking to school may be far less emphasized than it might be in a personal-experience essay, but touching on activities like that can help to ground a work—that is, give it a foundation.

Another technique is to focus on a contrast of feelings or emotions. If you are exploring attitudes toward old age, for example, it might be effective to contrast how you felt as a child and your attitude now. Or if street violence is your general topic, you might consider turning your attention back and forth between the mother of a gang member and her son.

There is a third approach to the reflective essay that is, as I have suggested, actually very close to poetry: selecting an **image**—something you see, touch, or hear—and using it as a vehicle for discussing your true concern. This is precisely the approach used by Jackson Jodie Daviss' reflective piece "Stone's Throw."

With this in mind, read this essay through once for pleasure and a second time for analysis from a writer's point of view. You will draw much more from the essay if you write marginal comments during the second reading.

Stone's Throw

by Jackson Jody Daviss

I was washing my rock with strong soap and a stiff brush when I realized it isn't my rock. Nonetheless, I continued to scrub it clean and pat it dry, and I will use it. It's one of the better rocks I've come across, palm-sized, with a nice heft to it, a pleasing band of white quartz sandwiched between gray granite halves, and one good flat spot. The flat spot is necessary because the rock will be a paperweight, and paperweights shouldn't roll. And, as it will be weighing down papers important to me, I had good reason to clean the rock before putting it to use. But of course, it's not my rock.

I don't know much about rocks, but I do know that most of them have been around a lot longer than I have. It might be possible to argue for the youth of some lava rock, the newly solidified lava from currently active volcanoes. But isn't that really old rock that was melted then reconstituted? It seems then, all rocks have a few years on me.

This particular rock is so old that time and events have worn it into a smooth, if irregular, ovoid. Most probably it spent long years in fast-flowing water, having its edges rolled and pounded away. But that's not where I found it. Somehow it had traveled to the edge of a parking lot in Bangor, Maine. How long it had been parked there, leading a presumably idle existence, is anybody's guess. The rock has been knocking around, by my measurement, just short of forever. Its future stretches into an equally unimaginable time span, certainly exceeding that allotted to me. Clearly, such an aged, ageless rock will never be mine—or anyone else's. This realization was difficult for me, forced as I was to admit I could lay no claim to something even after giving it a good bath. With me, familiarity often breeds possessiveness.

For what will be a brief chapter in the history of this rock, it will be used by me to help keep track of my written work, used perhaps 50 years, if I live that much longer and don't lose the rock. (Then again, can a rock be lost? If so, when is it home? Where does it belong, who'd miss it and who'd remember it by the time it got back? Furthermore, does a rock ever miss the old neighborhood? What if the quarry is now a swimming hole, and home is under 30 feet of water? It may be true for rocks as it is for the rest of us—you can't roll home again.)

The preceding parenthetic rambling is a fine example of what's known as going off on a tangent, something else with which I'm intimately familiar. What I really need is a paperweight of the mind. Scraps of scattered thoughts and bits of ideas grow and shift and edge each other out, endlessly rearranging their strata. And, because my desk top is a reflection of my state of mind, my notes and rough drafts habitually reshuffle themselves into disorder when I'm not looking.

The rock's strata, though, are bonded solidly in order; I'm hoping this paperweight might have an osmotic stabilizing influence on both mind and matter. Best not to expect too much, I suppose, keeping in mind the old saying that you can't get blood out of a stone; it's probably no easier to get peace of mind from a rock. I'll try to be satisfied if all it does is keep track of my papers, because, although this rock has undoubtedly held a series of steady positions, this may after all be its first job.

This rock will serve its sentry duty along with a large pair of broken scissors, a cracked stoneware mug, an empty Lancers bottle and other weighty objects, all of which will surely outlast me, though not by as much as the rock. In fact, the contents of the Lancers bottle was one of the few things more fleeting than the writer who drank it.

These musings on mortality bring me, finally, to thoughts on the transitory nature of writing. Will any of my works, in print or in the reader's memory, survive as long as, say, the half-life of an empty Lancers bottle? Probably not.

So why bother? Why does any writer bother? Two major reasons are fear and hope: fear that you won't get what you want except through writing; hope that you will get what you want, precisely through writing. Which attitude gets the emphasis depends on whether the writer sees a bottle as half empty or half full. As it happens, after draining the Lancers bottle, I thought of myself as half full and the bottle as having further possibilities. So, I'm a writer who hopes, and my hopes are the common ones.

There is the hope of being published, thereby furthering the cycle of this particular form of self-expression by reaching an audience. And there is the inherent potential for influencing that audience. And there is the hope—in this line of work, it amounts to more of a wish—for financial gain. Or it could be the old vain hope for immortality. Maybe, after all the paper and people have crumbled to ashes, this rather pleasing rock, again well-covered in dust (perhaps my own), will remember me. And maybe, tell a sedentary comrade, "You know, hers was one of the better first novels I've ever held down."

It could be the only good review I ever get, but that one would be set in stone.

• • • •

Marginal Notes That Help

What kind of marginal notes are helpful? Approaches vary. Some are brief, others are extensive; some are in the margins (if there's room), others are kept in notebooks. What follows is one of many different styles of reading notes. Don't be upset if your approach is quite different. This isn't a test. What *is* important is the principle of active, analytical reading.

The excerpts from Daviss' essay are the type that should attract your attention, and the brief indented comments in italics are the sort that might prove helpful.

> I was washing my rock with strong soap when I realized it isn't my rock.
> *Grabs attention. A good hook.*

> . . . a pleasing band of white quartz sandwiched between gray granite halves, and one good flat spot.
> *Very specific details. Significant?*

> But of course, it's not my rock.
> *Repeated phrase. Could be important.*

> It seems then, all rocks have a few years on me.
> *Understatement. Keeps the tone light.*

> How long had it been parked there, leading a presumably idle existence, is anybody's guess.
> *Comic phrasing. Conversational.*

With me, familiarity often breeds possessiveness.
A twist on the cliché.

Then again, can a rock be lost? If so when is it home? Where does it belong. . . .
Clever phrasing—but where's the focus?

I'm hoping this paperweight might have an osmotic stabilizing influence on both mind and matter.
"Osmotic" like "osmosis"? Maybe learning gradually.

These musings on mortality bring me, finally, to thoughts on the transitory nature of writing.
The theme?

So why bother? Why does any writer bother?
Good question! Will she answer it?

There is hope of being published [and] . . . reaching an audience. And there is the hope . . . of financial gain . . . or the old vain hope for immortality.
Positive reasons for writing.

And, maybe, tell a sedentary comrade, "You know, hers was one of the better first novels I've held down."
It could be the only good review I ever get, but that one would be set in stone.
Ends with a pun!

Summary: A serious piece about mortality & reasons why we write. Rock is immortal, we aren't. We write lit. anyhow. Tone stays light. Puns, comic metaphors, etc.

Wordplay: Metaphors Puns, Symbolic Stones

"Stone's Throw" is similar in one respect to "The Hip Plumber" in Chapter 11. The tone in both essays is light, often comic, but the themes in both are serious. In "Plumber," however, the comedy is character driven. That is, the humor comes from incongruities in the character himself. In "Stone's Throw," the humor is language driven. It's verbal humor. Incidentally, those two terms, *character driven* and *language driven,* are helpful in analyzing any humorous work from Shakespeare's comedies (he uses both) to the routines of contemporary standup comics.

One of Daviss' stylistic techniques is understatement. While geologists refer to the age of rocks as being in the millions of years, Daviss merely points out that "most of them have been around a lot longer than I have." Later she observes that "all rocks have a few years on me." (If you listen carefully to the humor of young people, you will discover that **overstatement**—exaggeration is the preferred approach among children, while an appreciation of understatement comes, if at all, with maturity.)

Whimsical metaphors are another characteristic of her style. She describes herself as disorganized and in need of "a paperweight of the mind." Her meaning is perfectly clear (many of us have searched for the same), but translating that phrase into nonmetaphorical language is not easy. We might explain it by saying that she needs something to keep her focused, but "focus" is a metaphor too—and much less original. Or we might say that she wants to "keep on track," but that's a cliché. Her metaphor is both unique and clear.

Later she states that the rock as a paperweight "will serve its sentry duty along with a large pair of broken scissors" and other objects on her desk. Sentries? It's a cartoon image, but again we know immediately what she means.

Personification is a popular device in poetry, but you may not have realized that it is a specialized form of metaphor. When we write "the angry sea" we are suggesting that the ocean is acting "like an angry person." Daviss' rock as a sentinel keeping order on her desk is far more original. And so is the metaphor that concludes the essay. Here the rock becomes a wise old critic who announces, "hers was one of the better first novels I've held down."

Puns are vastly underrated in our age. We often respond to them with groans rather than laughter. But they were highly regarded by the Elizabethans. Even the melancholy Hamlet couldn't resist them from time to time. Nor can the not-so-melancholy Daviss. "This rock," she tells us, "has undoubtedly held a series of steady positions." This is a personification, suggesting that the rock will now take on "its first job"; but "positions" applies not only to it's *vita* (assuming a rock has a life) but also to its literal state lying prone on the ground. And you probably noticed how at the end of the essay the rock, personified again, makes his critical comment to "a sedentary comrade," one who is both inactive and, by nature, sedimentary.

There is one more whimsical use of language that deserves a close look. Every writing class stresses the need to avoid **clichés**. But some rather good writers from Shakespeare to Dylan Thomas have enjoyed resurrecting a number of the most disreputable clichés either by rephrasing them or placing them in a fresh context. Daviss reawakens four different clichés in this short essay. We all know the overused phrase "Familiarity breeds contempt," but Daviss jolts it into life by describing her attitude toward rocks she finds and keeps with the phrase "Familiarity breeds possessiveness." Later she uses the shopworn phrase "can't get blood out of a stone" without alteration. She brings it to life by applying it to an actual stone that she has found. She has turned a tired **figure of speech** into a literal statement. The same is true of "seeing life as a glass half empty" (the pessimist) "or half full" (the optimist). Again, she applies the phrase literally to that bottle of Lancers wine. She even uses a wellworn phrase in the concluding sentence:

> It could be the only good review I ever get, but that one would be set in stone.

If this sentence were used in an essay that did not refer to stones at all, the phrase "set in stone" would be a cliché similar to "etched in stone." But now that we have come to know her paperweight almost as a friend, albeit a sedentary one, this final critical note becomes the bitter-sweet reward for the writer.

When we examine these verbal gymnastics one by one, each in isolation, it may seem that this essay is just light entertainment. But if you look closely at the symbolic use of that stone, you will see that the theme is as weighty as granite. As writers, we have a secret hope that our work will endure through the ages. This motivates us to put in long hours perfecting our art in what the author describes as "the old vain hope for immortality." But a chilly voice of reason reminds us that neither we nor our works will last forever. Rocks are immortal; we and our writing are not. This realization can lead us to depression, that half-empty wine bottle, or to determination and confidence, the half-full bottle. Themes like this are heavy stuff.

One final note: meticulous close reading sometimes seems to take the fun out of an essay like this, so before we move on, read the piece once more just for enjoyment. Analysis is essential for full appreciation, but don't let it upstage pleasure.

An Essay for Discussion

The next essay, "Total Laryngitis," by Trinie Dalton, is reserved for discussion. You're on your own. Here are some aspects worth considering when going through your second reading.

Like Daviss' piece, this work is reflective. It moves freely from one thought to the next. There is a unifying element, but it is different from the approach Daviss uses. Compare and contrast the ways these two essays establish a sense of order.

Clearly this is not a medical report. Just how is the author using laryngitis? What does it represent?

The essay moves from one simile to another. Each suggests a slightly different feeling. Pick out a few and analyze what they imply.

The Asian woman crossing the street seems to be important. She isn't a metaphor—why? But she is significant—how?

In the last paragraph Dalton makes many contrasts between items that are two-dimensional and those that are three-dimensional. See if you can explain each of those references.

Look closely at that very last sentence. What does it refer to (easy), and what does it suggest (more challenging)?

Take a close look at the style. Dalton's writing violates just about every rule ever suggested for good English. How would you describe her use of language? (Pick out particular examples.) Is it justified?

Total Laryngitis

by Trinie Dalton

Not being able to talk feels like you are riding on the wing of an airplane through the mist of feathery, stratospheric clouds, and it's so cold and desolate, and you're trying to tap the thick double layers of the 747's passenger windows with your shortcut fingernails, beads of water bulging on your tonsils, and then it's better to just shut up.

Hello. I have total laryngitis. Lean over to hear me whisper hoarsely into your ear. My inner ear is submerged in an ocean of echoes, but if you whisper back to me it will sound like wind in a cave and make me feel coy, like a baby possum. Now are the days to share secrets. There's a blanket that my grandmother made that has orange, green, blue, and pink cotton yarn woven into netting, making a fabric that can cover or expose you—take your pick. Poke your fingers and toes through if you're hot, or jumble the soft sections into a pile that protects your ears, hair, and cheeks if the outside is giving you the chills. Laryngitis is similar to this crafty network of ruffled grandma flowers—oblivion at the edge of oblivion. Did you hear that? I *said*, laryngitis is similar to this crafty network of ruffled grandma feathers—oblivion at the edge of *what?*

Lust is one effect of this illness. Because when two people are whispering phrases back and forth, there is a tendency to watch lips move, to watch the teeth appear and disappear, and to feel the steamy breaths gathering in your deep ear's spiral cochlea forming dew droplets, like the dew that the fairies drink in the night-scented garden of jasmine, gardenia, and the favorite blossoms of moths. Kissing may not be the best idea due to germs, but the intimacy of silence can be better than sex. Eye contact is a key factor in the reverse nighttime that the quiet proposes; noise is absent, but light and touch still exist.

And back to the knitted blanket that grandma made, lust and this blanket lend themselves perfectly to one another, they illustrate perfect union when you can hide with someone under a blanket and whisper and giggle and tell secrets. Maybe that's juvenile, but maybe that's just plain great. Yeah, I know that people don't easily reveal their innermost desires, but I imagine if there was some method to coax the secret wax out of them it would be all about getting covered up in granny's blankets and laughing with friends. It would be about feeling huddled like puppies and thinking they were in on something that the rest of the world was clueless to. People dig secrets. People love to feel included. The best part about total laryngitis is that it's a flashlight into a cavern of warm, toasty security because you know that the people you're whispering to actually care to hear what you're saying.

An Asian woman in a Graff polyester blouse, sweat pants, and red high heels is crossing in the crosswalk at Santa Fe Ave. and 38th St. Her frizzy, perm-damaged hair is bouncing up and down in the wind as if it's one big chunk of hard cheese. Her smile, defined by the arc of her Maybelline red lips, dissolves the smog from lanes of traffic crowded with big rigs. Industrial area. It's like, her teeth are so extremely white that you see them from a quarter-mile away, beaming gleefully despite the wafting scents of salty lard from a nearby rendering plant. Her happiness strips all the shit away, and that's exactly NOT how total laryngitis is. When you can't talk, you feel like burning this whole lady scenario up like the rejected negative of a potentially too-brilliant photograph. If there were a lighter in the pocket of your Levi's, you would get it out, and set everything on fire to symbolize your total disgust with not being able to sing and be gay like that woman crossing the street.

Every few hours, though, there are fleeting thoughts of positivity, thoughts that remind you that total laryngitis may be total momentarily, but it isn't total for a lifetime. What is total, really? Sleeping, eating, that's all. And those are riddled with variables. Total laryngitis is one of those variables: extra sleep becomes a must, and the diet becomes specialized, because it hurts to eat crunchy foods. Anyway, daily life amidst the city's noise, pitted against the astounding personal silence that equals space travel in a claustrophobic capsule with nothing to do but count boxes of dehydrated pastas and freeze-dried ice creams, is disorienting. So when there's a minute of up, of believing that your voice will someday make a mighty return like a cowboy riding up over a sand dune in Monument Valley, there's a reason to rejoice. You hear the horse's hooves shuffling softly through piles of red sand. You try to talk, like the disease has ended or it's psychosomatic, but nothing comes out. Crackling low-volume vibrations make your mouth itch enough to cough or wheeze.

Why do we compare feelings of isolation with being launched into space, for example, the airplane wing or space capsule mentioned before? Maybe loneliness is more similar to receiving a fax of someone else's voice copied flat onto a sheet of shiny, curled fax paper. Or, that's probably more like being deaf. Okay, you send out postcards of your voice, you address a mailer to every friend you have that says, "Hello! I want to talk!" But when they get it, they think it's junk mail and throw it away with the Pizza Hut coupons. They don't understand the cryptic language of the mute, the encoded data that means, "Please hear me." It looks like advertisement, the clutter that no one has time for. Even some of your closest friends are too busy to tolerate, listen, and concentrate in order to learn your new language. They aren't interested in the dilemma of being misunderstood.

How does the voice become two-dimensional? A voice minus sound is two-dimensional, it becomes a postcard of itself. A picture of somewhere you've visited before, remember fondly, and would like to return to. But human character is not made up of postcards; humans are multi-dimensional and our collective voices make a song. Voice music is 3D, and is animated. Rocks are 3D but they are inanimate, and total laryngitis is like being a river stone: a lot passes you by and you rub what you can. I prefer being an animated 3D version of myself, because then I feel like a cartoon superhero flying through life. When total laryngitis leaves, I'll re-upholster my couch and then rearrange my furniture with my improved vocal abilities. I'll bake brownies by speaking to the chocolate in the mixing bowl. The new red Maybelline I bought will look good on my lips.

15

A SENSE OF PLACE

"On Leaving Florida" by Marjorie Sandor. Sights, sounds, and smells. The historical context. The author's emotional involvement. An essay for discussion: "The Rise and Fall of Rodney" by Jack Bertram.

On Leaving Florida

by Marjorie Sandor

In early June, Newnans Lake is a glossy mud-green, the color of secrets. I take another step deeper in and cast my dry fly, a 12 Yellow Humpy made in Montana, toward a faint dimpling twenty feet out, though any rise around here is as likely to be an alligator as a fish. They say there are a couple thousand gators in this lake, and as I cast, one of them groans hoarsely in the mangroves behind me. My fishing companion, a colleague from the nearby University of Florida who takes pleasure in testing an outsider's mettle—especially a *girl's*—explains that two big people standing in the water will send any self-respecting gator the other way. But I'm not big, and not convinced. Only my torso is currently above water; choice bits are below, and my companion chooses this moment to realize *all of a sudden* that he's left his grass shrimp on the tailgate of his truck. He thrashes off through the water toward the mangroves, and that, as the nursery rhyme goes, "leaves only one."

I'm beginning to doubt the wisdom of my quest to gain Florida *machisma,* but after six years here, my husband and I will be moving to the West, and this looks like my last chance to get a glimpse of the real Florida. Ever since we decided to move to Oregon, I've felt twinges of regret in advance, a disturbing mix of relief and shame over my failure to acclimatize. So when my colleague, a native Floridian, agreed to take me fishing one last time, it seemed like a requisite ceremony, the divestiture of a failed initiate.

In fact, the conditions he set bore all the marks of a ceremonial dressing-down. "Take off those damn hip waders," he said. "And that fishing vest, too—we'll have none of that fancy shit." And so on: I would have to wade in

111

my shorts. I could tote my fly rod and a couple of flies if I must, but I'd better be prepared to put grass shrimp on the end of my tippet if I really wanted to catch fish. I submitted, and now here I stand, perfectly alone, my legs numb, as if they've been anesthetized prior to amputation. Still, this guy seems to know the region's secret places, its guarded heart, lushly complex and easily maddened; like it or not, he's my last-minute guide to a paradise faintly familiar and more than faintly inimical.

*

The familiar is simply this: at first, the city of Gainesville, in the north central region of the state, reminded me of my hometown in southern California, a place I hadn't lived—or known I had missed—for over fifteen years. Even the weekend of the job interview, I felt keenly a sense that any minute I might round a corner and happen onto a street I knew. Maybe it was the palms and live oaks, the historic Thomas Hotel with its red-tiled roof and fountains and borders of azaleas, or the orange groves and horse pastures outside the city limits, which reminded me dimly of pictures I'd seen of the San Gabriel Valley before development, with its great ranchos and groves of orange trees. But my nostalgia was rimmed with suspense, for here there were coral snakes and alligators, sticky vines curling under window frames, and cockroaches the size of baby mice. In the rainy season, chairs and books were lightly veiled in green. Even the produce looked different to me: okra, in particular, shocked me a little with its velvety fuzz, its fantastic pearls-and-slime within. Here was the sensuality of the deeply native—inviting, then rejecting, the stranger.

My husband and I were living in Boston at the time, and apart from the fact that it was winter and our teaching jobs were temporary, I believe I applied for the Florida position out of curiosity. I went to the campus interview blindly, cheerfully, without even consulting a map, the way you might go to a movie without seeing the preview. All I had to go on was a brief burst of enthusiasm from the university's creative writing program director (himself a Yankee) when he telephoned to arrange the visit.

"We've got great bird life," he cried. "And you don't need a sweater."

So the seduction began. When I stepped off the plane in Gainesville, it was mid-January and seventy degrees, the air itself some rare form of bliss. The director ushered me swiftly into his ancient sage-gray Pontiac the color of Spanish moss, and announced that we were going straight to "the Devil's Millhopper." I thought he was making a joke about the interview process, but no, he was in fact referring to a natural phenomenon—a 120-foot-deep sinkhole where the limestone substrata had caved in. As I stepped carefully down the dappled trail in my interview shoes, I couldn't fight the pleasurable incongruity of those fancy black pumps moving down and down into a green funnel of magnolia, dogwood, violets, and ferns, with little springs running out of its steep sides to form a small pool below. As we stood at the bottom, remote from sunlight, an iridescent blue lizard hesitated, oracular, on my shoe.

That night, after the interview, I called my husband and told him what I'd seen that day: a huge flock of sandhill cranes; egret and ibis and great blue heron; a big shimmery blue-black bird called the anhinga, perched on a cypress stump with its wings spread wide to dry. Alligators, armadillos, little country stores, and huge trees right in town. "It smells good here," I said. "And you don't need a sweater."

And he: "If they offer, take it."

*

Back in Boston, we prepared for our new life as if we were going on an exotic adventure-vacation, buying new cameras, maps and guidebooks, and flimsy tropical-theme shirts. We were, I see now, simply an updated version of the naive American settler, the kind who not all that long before us headed into the unknown with parakeet and piano and joyous misconception, only to pitch the whole lot out the back of the wagon months later.

But not yet: even as the close heat of our first summer descended, the seductive nostalgia I'd felt on my first visit held me fast. The birdsong of my California childhood pierced the neighborhood quiet at dawn and dusk: raucous jays, the manic repertoire of mockingbirds, the cool triplicate sighs of mourning doves. The Spanish had come to the west coast of North America as they'd come here, in search of fabled golden cities and unfathomable wealth, and who could blame them? It seemed appropriate, and a little spooky, that Ponce de Leon named Florida before he actually landed. "Isle of Flowers," he apparently said as he sighted land from the deck of his fragile caravel in 1513. Back home in Spain, they were celebrating the Feast of Flowers, and he believed the place to be an island, so ultimately the name is built entirely out of wish, mistake, and the memory of home—for what else do we have at times of discovery? Once landed, how shocked he must have been by the mysteries of the actual.

Someone urged us to buy a canoe: this was the best way to explore the wilderness. This statement is not untrue. It's just more precise to say that the canoe gives Florida a chance to explore *you*. On our first trip down the Suwanee River, I recall, we were leaning back in the silky air, taking in the hypnotic buzz of insects and the still lifes of turtles on logs, and saying to each other, *I'll bet this is what Eden was like*—when that primitive fish, the alligator gar with its long snout and studded spine, leaped up into the air and slapped itself down in our boat like a curse. It took us about twenty minutes to get it out of the canoe, with Sisyphean hoists of the paddle, until at last we tumbled it, thrashing, over the side. Our nerves were shot, but the day wasn't over: a few minutes later I went off into the woods to take a pee and discovered, at my feet, a cottonmouth moccasin—dead, as it turned out, but who can escape that first impression?

Whenever we canoed on a spring creek with our daughter, we held her tight against our own desire to leap into that water, so limpid and full of light, a dazzling turquoise wherever the springs bubbled up through the limestone. A simple, perfectly safe outing, you'd think, if it weren't for the little white signs posted at intervals: BEWARE! ALLIGATORS. BEWARE! RABID OTTERS.

Still, we saw great blue heron lifting heavily out of reeds, the sudden launch and twist of a red mullet three feet into the air, the long springcreek runs with their water hyacinths and freshwater grasses rippling out under the surface—a Monet run amok. For a while we lived eleven miles south of Gainesville in the town of Micanopy, a village of rutted sand roads and persimmons hanging low enough to pluck without stretching at all. Our neighbor George, a rangy and generous woodworker, kept his studio's backdoor open so anybody could wander on up anytime. His tables and lampstands were curved and sinuous, not unlike the snakes he said were "on the move" in the spring, looking for mates. He warned us pleasantly to stay alert: one of them might, at any moment, drop right out of a tree. It was George who told us the history of the place: how it had been inhabited longer than anyone knew, starting with the Timuacuans, a sun-worshiping people here long before the Spanish conquest. The town itself was named for the Seminole chief Micanope, who refused, along with Osceola and four other chiefs, to sign the treaty of Payne's Landing. Osceola himself had once made a bold attack on the fort here. George told us also about the two gods of the Florida Seminole: Ishtoholo, the Great Spirit, and Yo-He-Wah, the one who commands devils and brings catastrophe—and whose name cannot be spoken in daily life, only chanted during ceremonies at which he is appeased with dances and sacrifices.

"Have you noticed yet?" George asked. "You dream pretty strange when you sleep on so many Indian graves."

Driving back and forth between Gainesville and Micanopy, on old Highway 44 that cuts across Payne's Prairie, I once saw a sunset that made me think of that split Seminole spirit. The sunset was one that only Florida can produce: half of it a row of delicate shell-pink wisps, the other half all fire and flame, like the first Technicolor documentary of a volcano. Two skies in one place, like the two sides of a human face in an old tintype, where one half is full of benign light and the other is brooding and sinister.

*

Maybe the end was inevitable. Within a year or two it was the violent sky that we began to see, a god grown too big in our minds. We had no rituals and nothing to sacrifice—only the futile modern lyric of complaint. On our explorations out of town, we awoke to more ugliness than beauty: the paper mills and huge tracts of quick-growing slash pine; the long, high fences surrounding the corrections facilities outside of town. Someone told us there were seventeen such institutions within a thirty-two-mile radius of Gainesville, and we repeated this statistic to ourselves with grim satisfaction. One year, a serial murderer made his nightly camp in the woods just outside of town, coming in to take the lives of five university students in shockingly theatrical displays. The Florida forest, filled with beauty and danger . . . took on another atmosphere in our imagination. It was a place to fear, a place that drew in solitary nature lovers who never came back—for reasons having nothing to do with wilderness.

*

There is, in the air over Newnans Lake this June day, the faint hush of a test being administered. I glance toward the mangroves to see if my colleague is ever coming back, and as I do, something long and silver vaults into the air like a knife thrown by a performing chef. Alligator gar, I'm pretty sure, but at the moment it hardly matters. I'm tingling all over, glad to be alive in this place that never stops surprising.

At last my companion emerges from the woods and joins me in the water. He looks a trifle disappointed that I'm still in one piece. We try the grass shrimp for an hour, but there's no action.

"It's not going to happen today—not here," he says in a way that chills me. "Let's get out of here."

It's his own property we retreat to, where he has a little sinkhole of his own, a pond he's stocked with bream and catfish and a couple of snapping turtles—along with a big old mudfish he swears got in there all by itself.

Watching me cast my Yellow Humpy, he sighs. I've got too much slack in my line and I don't know how to set the hook, but I catch bream after bream. "I can see you have the luck," he says, master of the derogatory compliment. "Let me see that thing." He takes the fly rod, lifts it high, and slams the Humpy down on the water, laying the line out perfectly straight, the fly perfectly placed at the edge of the duckweed. Then he yanks it back up so hard the water appears to boil, a tempest in a sinkhole. No fish.

I take the rod back, offering my hesitant beginner's casts—the equivalent of the lob in tennis, all height and no distance. This doesn't seem to matter to the catfish that comes blasting up from God-knows-where to take the fly.

As I leave my colleague's house, I hand him the ruined Humpy.

"Thanks," I say. "I'm going."

"Goodbye," he replies. "Good luck out there."

I wave a shaky goodbye and head for my car, keeping an eye on the sandy trail for the cottonmouth, the bejeweled and deadly coral snake. It's June, after all, and the snakes are once again on the move. There's a symphony of smells in the air: harmony and cacophony, everything at once. I can't describe it.

Could I, if I'd lasted longer? Years from now, out in Oregon, I'll still be trying to compose the scene: the nose-prickling fust of marsh, the dank rich of forest floor and the clean sharp lift of pine, the sweet weight of magnolia. I'll swear I smell the delicate orange, though I might be dreaming of that other grove I lost. There's no separating the smells of our remembered places, their skies, their dreams benign and sinister. This Florida, the Florida I'm leaving, won't leave me. It is the lush green vine of memory that grows in my nomad sleep, finding a way into the next wilderness I hope to call home.

• • • •

Sights, Sounds, and Smells

Creating a sense of place depends, above all else, on precise, fresh details. Most will be visual, but don't neglect the other senses.

Details have to take the form of nouns. Modifiers like "beautiful," "panoramic," and "awe-inspiring" or "bleak" and "desolate" don't in themselves create pictures. You can't see a "beautiful" or photograph a "desolate." Only things create pictures.

In addition, those sights, sounds, and smells have to be fresh and precise. One of the characteristics of routine travel pieces and brochures is the habitual use of overused words and outright **clichés** like "a tropical paradise," "a winter wonderland," "a land of contrasts," and "a Mecca for tourists." These are the junk food of hack writers.

In contrast, "Leaving Florida" provides a vast array of precise visual details. When they are modified, the adjective adds to the distinctiveness of the object described. In the opening sentence we are told that the lake is "a glossy mud-green." That's not just green. It is a particular shade and quality of green. When she first arrived in Florida, she thought perhaps it would look like California, but she soon discovered that here there were

> . . . coral snakes and alligators, sticky vines curling under window frames, and cockroaches the size of baby mice. In the rainy season, chairs and books were lightly veiled in green.

In this short passage there are five different visual details. Notice that those cockroaches are not described as "big" or "enormous." It's hard to make cockroaches more revolting than they are by nature, but comparing them with baby mice does it vividly.

In her first visit to a deep sinkhole she sees more pleasing sights:

> . . . a green funnel of magnolia, dogwood, violets, and ferns with little springs running out of its steep sides to form a small pool below. As we stood at the bottom, removed from the sunlight, an iridescent blue lizard hesitated, oracular, on my shoe.

The phrase "a green funnel" helps us to imagine descending into that 120-foot sinkhole. And the lizard is first individualized by being "iridescent blue" and then, perhaps because of its big eyes and solemn stare, made mysterious and wise like an oracle. How often have you seen a lizard described as "oracular"? That's what I mean by distinctive description.

These visual details pepper the entire essay straight through to the end when, on leaving, she watches her step on the "sandy trail" on the lookout for "the bejeweled and deadly coral snake." Even in that small detail she repeats the contrast between beauty and threat that has recurred throughout the essay, a pattern I will return to.

Sight, of course, is only one of five senses. This essay is unusual in the degree to which it also uses smells, sounds, and even the sense of touch. Take another look at this passage describing one of their canoe trips:

> . . . we were leaning back in the silky air, taking in the hypnotic buzz of insects and the still lifes of turtles on logs . . .

The feel of the air is "silky," a feeling like silk, a tactile **image**. "Hypnotic buzz" is for the ears. And the arrangement of turtles is like an artist's still-life painting. Three different senses in one sentence!

At the end of the essay she writes that even miles from Florida she will be trying to recapture the best that state had to offer. In this case she intensifies visual images with a highly original reference to smell:

> . . . I'll still be trying to compose the scene: the nose-prickling fust of marsh, the dank rich of forest floor and the clean sharp lift of pine, the sweet weight of magnolia.

You may not be familiar with "fust"—it's not in most dictionaries—but "fusty" is in common usage as that stale, musty smell that often comes from rotting trees. She gives you a hint with "dank rich of forest floor," combining it with the "sharp lift of pine," the scent rising. The writing here is as dense as it is in many poems; but if you read it carefully, all these lush odors create a vivid sense of being there.

The Historical Context

Distinctive places have distinctive histories. This is true of every geographic region in this country or abroad. Even a city block or an acre of farmland has a past. It is not always necessary to include the history of a place you are describing, but often it adds depth.

In "Leaving Florida" the author is careful to remind you that the area she is describing has a history that goes back far before the arrival of Europeans. Her friend George tells her:

> . . . how it had been inhabited longer than anyone knew, starting with the Timuacuans, a sun-worshiping people here long before the Spanish conquest. The town itself was named for the Seminole chief Micanope, who refused, along with Osceola and four other chiefs, to sign the treaty of Payne's Landing. Osceola himself had once made a bold attack on the fort here. George told us also about the two gods of the Florida Seminole: Ishtoholo, the Great Spirit, and Yo-He-Wah, the one who commands devils and brings catastrophe . . .

If you read the book, *The Night Gardener* (Lyons Press) from which this piece was excerpted, you will discover that the author has drawn on many such historical references. She quotes extensively from such writers as the 18th-century botanist William Bartram and the naturalist John Muir in the late 19th century.

Historical background requires research, and research takes time. But the computerization of library indexes and the Internet have made searches less arduous, sometimes even fun. For local places, regional historical societies can be helpful. And don't forget the contribution of long-time residents who may turn out to be living research centers.

One word of warning, however: extended quotations can stop the forward movement of your essay. As long as they illustrate a point you have made, they can serve. But if that point is forgotten, they may become an interruption rather than a contribution. Style is also a factor. Sometimes a quotation will provide valuable information but in a tedious way. Don't let a boring guest take over your narration with a dreary list of facts and figures.

If your historical background material begins to dominate, reexamine where you want your **focus**. Perhaps what started as an essay describing a particular place would be more effective as a historical account, the subject of the next chapter. There is no sharp line dividing the two types of essays, but it is important to determine which is your primary concern.

The Author's Emotional Involvement

Every literary nonfiction essay has a different degree of emotional involvement on the part of the author. We have seen how Connie Wieneke highlights her personal emotions in "Snakebit," developing not only her reactions to the event that occurred in her childhood but, equally, her **ambivalent** response to her mother. In contrast, James Houston never offers even a hint about his own feelings in "The Hip Plumber."

"On Leaving Florida" is one of those essays that, like "Snakebit," is deeply concerned with the author's feelings about the subject. The topic is Florida in both its benign and threatening aspects; but if you review the ending, you will see that we learn about the geographic area not through abstract description but through physical details and Sandor's personal feelings.

The essay also resembles "Snakebit" in the degree to which the emotional response is charged with an intense **ambivalence**. We are flooded with details that dramatize the natural beauty of the area, as when she is shown the sinkhole pool with its magnolias, dogwoods, violets, and ferns and the little blue lizard. She then telephones her husband to tell him about seeing the sandhill cranes, egrets, and herons. If these were the only details she provided, the essay would read like a pamphlet from the tourist office.

While her love of all those wonders remains with her, she is soon made aware of the threats from alligators, rabid otters, enormous roaches, and the gar "with its long snout and studded spine" that leapt into their canoe "like a curse." The dark side of the experience is further dramatized with paper mills, the 17 prisons in the area, and the serial murderer.

The essay is not divided into a positive view followed by some turning-point trauma that reveals all the horrors. Sandor's approach is much more subtle. She juggles the beauty and the ugly, clearly indicating that both are a part of this most unusual region.

Notice that even the people she describes suggest a full range from the woodworker, George, who is so trusting and generous that he leaves his studio's backdoor open to, at the other extreme, her fishing guide, who so curtly tells her what to wear and what kind of flies to use and then, to our delight, fails miserably.

This ambivalence remains with her even after she moves to Oregon. In retrospect, there is a slight tilt toward the "lush green vine of memory," but the essay as a whole has blended both the best and the worst. In short, Florida is not just a place for her, it has become a highly charged set of memories. You cannot separate her description of the area from her emotions about that region.

An Essay for Discussion

The essay that follows, "The Rise and Fall of Rodney," by Jack Bertram, is reserved for discussion. Although the writer is also a poet, he earns his living as a journalist. You will see this in the way he, like James Houston, keeps himself out of his essay.

Take a close look, however, at his attitude toward his subject. It is not entirely objective. What does he take seriously and what not so seriously?

Like all effective essays based on a specific place, he gives specific visual details. The ones he provides create a mood. Circle those that help you to see and experience this area.

Notice that he draws on historical background more than Marjorie Sandor does. This background is particularly important. Ask yourself what would be lost if he had not provided that view of the past.

Bertram makes more use of interviews with informants than Sandor does. What is his attitude toward them? Does his phrasing ever appear to echo their speech?

The Rise and Fall of Rodney

by Jack Bertram

The future of Rodney isn't pretty, but it's secure. There's a certain stability to the subtle shiftings of life in a ghost town.

No, this is not a place that rushes forward, and the handfuls of remaining residents generally reflect on the past, the near-mystical evaporation of the town's glory days, only when asked.

Lately, the asking has become more frequent.

The numbers of the curious are steadily increasing, with more and more strange pilgrims driving through the ragged town with their out-of-state tags and their disposable cameras, circling slowly, looking, looking, as if the answer to some cosmic question lay in the weeds and the rubble and the ruins.

They have heard how, in the years following the Civil War, the course of the mythic Mississippi changed, justlikethat, as if Gawd Awmighty suddenly reconsidered the atlas, shrugged, and crooked a finger, beckoning the flow of the river away from Rodney's landing, removing the water a good two miles from the docks of the booming port town, a city of commerce and churches and culture and crime.

These days, says Percy Emanuel, so many outlanders come to the ghost town that a Rodneyite could make a good living if he'd just put a Coke machine on his front porch.

"Every day," he says, "people drive 100 miles to see nothing."

Emanuel, 63, of Natchez, was raised in Rodney in the 1940s and '50s. Now, he comes for wild game.

He has purchased a 100-plus-year-old house that he is fixing up to use as camp quarters when he returns to stalk his 75 acres for whitetail deer in season.

At a glance, the wood-framed structure appears to be pure Tobacco-Road fare, a stack of timber topped by a rusted tin roof, the front porch supported by rough, knotty beams, the entire structure mounted on stilts of soft, ancient red brick.

Closer inspection, however, reveals how solid the place is and, inside, one can see how the windowpanes bear the bubbly waves of antique glass, and how the woodwork is heavy with heart cypress, including a hand-carved fireplace that, for the aged-home preservationist, is history to die for.

"It don't warp," says Emanuel.

Heart cypress beats the elements, he says.

Emanuel's "new" house—he bought it about two years ago—is on the river side of the surviving town "square," which is maybe two, maybe three, city blocks long, by contemporary standards.

The river side of Rodney—the banks of which have progressed over the decades to about 8 miles from the Mississippi—is opposite the square from the locked-up Presbyterian Church, which was erected in 1830–31 and is an official landmark, listed on the National Register of Historic Places.

A Civil War cannonball is lodged in the brick above the front door. Scattered across the church lawn, among the waist-high weeds, are several historical markers, weed-tall metal tablets on pedestals, like toadstools, with narratives on topics such as "History of Rodney—Her Rise" and "Old Town of Rodney—Structures."

Freda Piazza, who moved to Rodney in 1941 when she married at the age of 20, likes to tell the story of how, during the Civil War, a Rodney belle supposedly hid a Union sailor under her hoop skirts in that place of worship, how today a painted "X" marks the spot in the chapel.

The Federals from the gunboat *USS Rattler* had come ashore to attend services at the church when they were surprised by Rebel raiders.

Legend has it that the Yankee sailor returned after the war and married his savior, says Piazza.

The story is one of several she recounts in *A Lifetime of Shenanigans,* a self-published, 267-page, book-bound "letter" to her children and grandchildren that, naturally, includes much about her "hometown" ghost town, although in the early years she split time between Rodney and nearby Fayette.

"Rodney was not exactly the best place in the world for a 20-year-old newlywed to be," Piazza writes in her memoir.

Even then, "the majority of its citizens were elderly . . . (people) who resisted the ravages of time and changes that converted Rodney from a . . . robust river town to a ghost town."

But hers has been a good life in Rodney, says Piazza.

She is the wife of the late Salvo (Salvatore) Piazza, a rancher, merchant and game warden for Jefferson County. Their life was forged on acreage a mile down the road from the town proper, where today Piazza lives in a comfortable, contemporary, ranch-style house, a stark architectural contrast to the relics and restorations, the few new structures, the outbuildings and the mobile homes that dot the heart of the ghost town.

At the square, there are an old wooden fraternal lodge building and grocery store, and there are a couple of other old brick buildings, both in disrepair, one a former store where the merchants resided on the top floor, and the other a one-teacher schoolhouse for the white children.

There are two churches, each more than 100 years old, each painted white, each still in use today. They are the churches, one Baptist, one Methodist, of the remaining black residents.

The tiny Zion Chapel AME Church is in the back yard of Daisy McGill, 83. McGill says she does not know how old the Zion church is and that the chapel was not originally located in her back yard, although it has been there for as long as she can remember, which is back to 1936, when she moved into the wood frame house. It, too, had been there for decades by that time.

She estimates that today, there are about 20 families that call Rodney home, although the number is hardly carved in stone. She can remember well, she says, the days when the fields to the north and west of her house were covered with residences.

And "there was a good store," says McGill. "You didn't have to go out of Rodney for nothing." There were also a post office and a jailhouse, she says.

The white folks had a dance hall where "the big bands came in" to play, while the blacks "had the jukes."

Most of the black residents, who "worked by the day," left when the farmers started using motorized equipment in the 1900s, she says, while the big exodus of both blacks and whites came after World War II.

Today, several hunt clubs have invaded, inhabiting the old buildings and setting up mobile homes. One sporting group utilizes a railroad car for quarters.

McGill says the hunters call her "the mayor of Rodney."

For Camella Richardson, Rodney was a historical amusement park, sans the carnival trappings.

Richardson, 50, is Piazza's daughter, and she remembers her youth in Rodney as an adventure akin to "going back into the 1800s."

It was not uncommon, she says, to see people traveling the roads by wagon, and she distinctly recalls the old country store with the proverbial pot-bellied stove at its social center, and the neighbor with the wall-mounted hand-crank telephone.

Richardson's childhood explorations took her inside most of the abandoned structures and, in the unkempt cemetery in the gothic, eroding bluffs above the Presbyterian Church, she would find Civil War artifacts and play in a trench that was dug by Rebel soldiers for use as a rifle pit.

The familiar scenery of her youthful environs included two hand-hewn log buildings on the Piazza property that the family, fearing the structures would eventually rot, sold to preservationists who relocated the structures to other sites in the state. Piazza, an avid hunter and outdoorswoman (her son, Mike, is the county game warden today), says, "I used to want to see development" in Rodney. "Now, I don't want to see anything developed."

She has become a traveler, having visited all 50 states and several foreign countries, and she does not care for the so-called progress she has seen on many of her journeys.

Piazza still writes an occasional historical piece on Rodney for *Bluffs & Bayous,* a Natchez publication.

"Next I want to write an article just on the sounds of Rodney," she says, smiling. "No motorcycles, no train whistles . . . "

The grin widens as she recalls one of those country-store, winter gatherings around the centerpiece wood stove, when one of the old men in the group stopped his rocking and humming and suddenly announced, "Here we are in Rodney, waiting on time to die."

16

A GLIMPSE OF HISTORY

Objective versus personal approaches. What to look for. "Captain Hind the Highwayman" by C. V. Wedgwood. Research and more research. Defining your topic. Organizing your material. Determining your tone. An essay for discussion: "The Key" by Stephen Minot

Objective versus Personal Approaches

The two essays in this chapter illustrate two significantly different approaches to writing about historical events. C. V. Wedgwood is a distinguished British historian specializing in the 17th century. Her work always reflects a deep, even personal concern for her subject, but like many traditional scholars she rarely uses "I" or reveals her emotional reactions directly. Although we recognize her writing as unmistakably literary because of her use of language and her flashes of wry humor, what we learn about her personal feelings is revealed only indirectly through implications.

In contrast, my essay, "The Key," is highly subjective. At first reading it may seem as if it should be classified as a memoir. It records personal experience and, unlike Wedgwood's work, is presented in the first person. But although the episode is autobiographical, the theme is not. Its primary concern is not the author but aspects of the 1960s civil rights movement and questions about the challenges ahead.

What to Look For

"Captain Hind," like most works of literary nonfiction, calls for two readings at least. The first is strictly for enjoyment. The exploits of historical figures in the Robin Hood tradition are always entertaining. In your second reading, however, take a close look at how Wedgwood has defined her topic. If you review the opening and closing paragraphs, you will see how precisely she has done this. Next, study the way she has organized her material. Notice that within the story line there are blocks of background information, including flashbacks.

123

Finally, take a close look at the style, especially those subtle hints about the author's personal feelings. There is even one uncharacteristic, and revealing, use of the pronoun "I." You will draw much more from this essay if you consider these three areas on your own before reading the analysis that follows.

Captain Hind the Highwayman

by C. V. Wedgwood

There was a noisy arrest one November morning in 1651 at a barber's shop opposite St. Dunstan's Church in Fleet Street. The news spread quickly through the neighbouring alleys so that Captain Hind the Highwayman had a large public when he was brought out, manacled, thrust into a waiting coach and carried off to the Council of State at Westminster. Highwaymen did not, as a rule, command the attention of the Government and I like to think that the dapper little man, as he entered on the last phase of his notorious career, had the gratification of knowing that he had achieved something.

The highwayman proper, as distinguished from the ordinary robber, footpad and the other minions of the moon[1] known to Shakespeare, was new to the annals of English crime. The word itself, significantly, begins to occur only during the general relaxation of law and order which accompanied the outbreak of the Civil War in 1642. The armed horseman whose method was to force the wealthy traveller at the pistol's point to hand over his money was perhaps a natural outcome of that time. The highwayman needed steady nerves, firearms and a good horse, all things which a deserter, or a cashiered officer, might very well possess. Highwaymen were not, however, all of this class; indeed relatively few of them were, but the new technique which rapidly became as popular as it was effective was probably learnt from pioneers who had once been soldiers. Sometimes they operated alone, more often in gangs. Many, if not all of them, pretended to a sort of Robinhoodishness. The only prey worth their while were the rich but they made a kind of virtue of this necessity and for that reason, perhaps, were popular, in theory at least, among the poor.

James Hind was one of the first to mark the profession with the strong imprint of his character. His gaiety, his daring, his Royalist sympathies and elegant manners were the familiar talk of inn-keepers and ostlers on every main road. He had 'pranced the road' from London to York, was well known to Gloucestershire, the Fens and the Thames valley and had, with his gang, at one time, levied almost regular tribute on the travellers who came to London by way of Barnet Heath.

Fame is not healthy for a highwayman and after a few years Hind fled the country, lurked in the Netherlands, dodged across Ireland and arrived in Scotland just in time to be presented to the young Charles II—who had a weakness

---

[1] Those who work by moonlight.

for clever scoundrels—and to enlist in the Royalist army as it set out to invade England. He saw action at Warrington and Worcester and after the King's defeat went to earth in the rabbit warren of London's most disreputable quarter.

Hind had ridden as a trooper in the King's army, but his public would not believe that their hero had played so small a part. It was widely rumoured that he had been Scoutmaster General and, when the young King eluded the pursuit of his enemies, it was to the skill and daring of Jemmy Hind that popular opinion attributed his escape.

The flattering rumour was Hind's undoing. Because they thought he might lead them to the King, the Government spared no pains in tracking him down. It was not Captain Hind the Highwayman but James Hind the Royalist whom the Council of State wished to see. The fugitive trooper from the King's defeated army would have been safe enough in London had he not trailed with him into his new profession those tell-tale clouds of glory from his past. His interview with the Council of State was a disappointment to both parties; he turned out to be of no importance to them at all.

Yet it hardly seemed sensible to release a public hero who had also been, in his time, a fairly considerable public nuisance. Direct evidence of his robberies was hard to come by, so he made his appearance at the Old Bailey about a month later on a charge of high treason.

Jemmy Hind was small and personable, with a confidence that did not overflow into swagger and gave him the easy air of a gentleman. A large audience had come to see and hear, hoping for some of his famous jests. The hearing, however, gave him few favourable openings for his wit and it was only at the end that he raised a laugh. Squinting down at his heels as he left the dock—'A plague on these great jingling spurs!' he said, and gave his irons a shake. Outside the crowd pressed upon him with lugubrious sympathy, asking him if he was to be hanged. 'No, no, good people,' he said, 'they are not in such a hurry to hang true folk.'

The fact was that they were not in such a hurry to hang a common thief on the distinguished charge of high treason. Evidence had come to light that, during his operations in Berkshire, he had once killed a man in a brawl; he was transferred to Reading and the charge was altered to manslaughter.

Under a medieval statute not yet repealed it was possible for any man who could read to avoid hanging for manslaughter by pleading benefit of clergy[2]; this reduced the penalty to a formal branding in the palm of the hand. Captain Hind in the dock at Reading was the same civil, witty, confident gentleman that he had been in London. But he had not realised that he would have to prove his right to benefit of clergy. He was utterly taken aback when a book was handed to him and he was told to read a paragraph. The gallant, play-actor's mask of gentility fell from his face: he could not read a word.

It was an eccentricity almost, for even in the humbler class from which he came, illiteracy was unusual. His father was an honest saddler of Chipping Norton who had wanted to make a scholar of his son; Hind had been two

---

[2]Members of the clergy and university students were subject to canon law rather than the harsher civil law.

years at school but his incorrigible 'waggishness' had prevented him from learning anything at all. Later he had been apprenticed to his father, and, when that did not please him, to a butcher; at the age of about eighteen he borrowed forty shillings from his doting mother and ran away to London.

Here he had fallen in with Allan, the boldest highwayman of his day, who used to disguise himself as a bishop, bowling along in his coach with outriders and servants. Once on a lonely stretch of road, off came the episcopal disguise, the coach was hidden behind a hedge and the gang took up their action stations. When, a little later, the bishop and his train reached the next town, they would listen with sympathy to the story of the robber band which had held up so many travellers that day and thank Heaven that the rogues had not molested them.

Young Hind learnt his profession and his good manners as gentleman usher to Bishop Allan and when Allan 'went to heaven in a piece of string' he set up on his own. The country was still disordered with echoes of civil war. Hind—one of the first gentlemen of the road to do so—adopted the title of Captain and permitted a general belief that he had served in that capacity for the King. His political views were, however, genuine; he robbed Parliament men[3] for preference and once, when he had robbed a poor Cavalier[4] in error, he not only gave him his money back, but dined with him at the next inn on the road, riding off at first light after paying the reckoning for them both. This was an act at once delicate and generous; Hind was a rogue but he was nature's gentleman.

There had been traces of grace and gallantry on the roads before Hind's time, but he was the first who made it a prevailing fashion. He never robbed without a jest and he always, with a little flourish, handed back to his victim a few shillings expenses money for the rest of his journey. In return he expected courtesy from his clients and when a traveller, for whom he had laid an ambush, came dawdling up at a foot pace, he whacked him smartly with his cane and cried 'Have I nothing to do all day but wait for you?'

His quick wits and resourcefulness gave rise to hundreds of tales. When he nipped a bag of gold out of a gentleman's coach at Hyde Park races, he got his booty safely through the London suburbs by waving it in the air as he galloped past, shouting, 'I've won my wager; I've won my wager.' The crowds made way for the jubilant victor and long before the pursuit came up with him, he had vanished.

Another time, when some of his victims were pelting along a dark highway after him, he ran into a happy, drunk parson, coming home from a wedding. Hind pressed his loaded pistol into his hand, breathlessly explaining that highwaymen were after him. Fire, he told the parson, and they'll away. The parson fired wildly, the pursuers took him for their robber, overpowered him and carried him off to prison, while Hind was already safe in the woods. The parson was, of course, a vile Puritan interloper; Hind the Cavalier would not have played such a prank on a priest of the Anglican church.

[3]Anti-Royalist followers of Oliver Cromwell.
[4]A Royalist supporter of Charles I.

True or false, the stories sprang from a genuine personality—the gay, civil gentleman who, in the dock at Reading, crumpled so pathetically into the saddler's truant son.

But his life was to end more nobly. While he waited for the hanging, Parliament passed an act of oblivion to cover crimes of violence committed during this disorderly epoch of the war. Hind was reprieved. But the authorities would not let so dangerous a thief escape. They revived the charge of high treason and transferred him from Reading gaol to Worcester. Here at the next assizes[5] he was tried and sentenced to be hanged for taking up arms for the usurper Charles Stuart. So, at last, on September 24th, 1652, Jemmy Hind the saddler's son joined the distinguished band of martyrs, knights, esquires, and peers of the realm who had mounted the scaffold for their King. He died if not exactly the death of a gentleman, yet a death that many gentlemen had not been ashamed to die.

• • • •

Research and More Research

If you are planning to write about a historical incident not based on personal experience, you will have to allow plenty of time for research. Almost always you will need a variety of sources. If you rely too heavily on just one, you run the risk of sounding imitative. In addition, you need a variety of material if you are going to determine your own unique approach.

If you have selected a recent event, interviews will help. Although Bertram's "The Rise and Fall of Rodney" is essentially a study of a particular place, it also contains historical events. He supplements visual impressions with interviews from more than one individual.

When the subject is farther back in history, you will have to rely on what others have written. Sometimes primary sources are available—statements or descriptions written by those who were there. If your topic is too far back for that, you will have to rely on secondary sources—information that is to some degree conjecture. Look at these sources carefully. Every writer has a different approach, and you won't want to accept one of these without weighing it carefully. If, for example, you are planning to write about the conduct of a Civil War general in a minor battle and your source describes him as incompetent, your work will be a mere echo of that position unless you can locate other views.

An essay like "Captain Hind" may look simple and straightforward, but notice how many different incidents are mentioned. Wedgwood is careful to differentiate information that seems certain and verifiable from that which may be an exaggeration or pure invention. She has an advantage of being exceptionally familiar with the historical period, but even if you can't match that level of expertise, you can learn a good deal through research. Gather as much information as you can, not just about your subject itself but the period as well.

[5]A trial session

Defining Your Topic

First, limit what you plan to cover. Then reduce even that. Most problems with essays on historical subjects stem from trying to include too much.

You can't do a biography of Winston Churchill in 10 pages. You can't even cover his early period in the Boer War. You will have to focus on one little-known and interesting incident that provides some fresh insight. In the same way, you can't describe the stock market crash of 1929. Concentrate instead on a crucial decision made by one individual in the space of a day or two. And no matter how fascinated you may be with mechanical engineering, you can't write a short paper about the building of the Brooklyn Bridge. Any attempt will sound like your seventh-grade efforts simply because you are skimming over the basic facts. You will have to limit your subject to one dramatic event on one specific day in that complex construction effort. You may find this process of limiting your topic frustrating, but there is greater agony in finding that you have wasted your time attempting the impossible.

Wedgwood's essay begins on "one November morning in 1651" and ends "on September 24th, 1652" when Jemmy Hind mounted the scaffold. Along the way, she provides background material about the instable times, his tutors in crime, and his cheerful failure as a student (a dramatic warning for high-school dropouts!); but the dates at the beginning and the end of the essay stand like bookends. Take a lesson from her: decide in advance just how much you can cover in the space available.

Organizing Your Material

Once you define the limits of your topic, consider jumping right in with action or dialogue. The formal introductory paragraph you may have used in grade school, and may still use for research papers, will not work well in literary nonfiction. Such introductions may inform readers, but they won't engage them. Traditional introductions are stiff and impersonal. Take another look at Wedgwood's opening: "There was a noisy arrest one November morning." Our interest is further focused in the next sentences: "The news spread quickly through the neighbouring alleys." This is history, but it has the impact of a short story.

After you have staked out the subject matter you plan to cover, consider more precisely what your opening and closing will be. This will help to keep you on track. The next step is to decide how much material you can include. If there are specific incidents that will dramatize your subject, consider one or more flashbacks. For a valuable review of that technique, take another look at Christopher Clausen's "Jack-in-the-Pulpit" (page 65) and Marjorie Sandor's "On Leaving Florida" (page 111). Keep in mind, however, that the shorter your work the more distracting shifts in time may be.

If organization strikes you as merely a mechanical consideration, remind yourself that you are not writing a utilitarian academic report. Your goal is to create literary nonfiction, a work that in addition to being informative is also a pleasure to read. You can allow yourself a bit more informality, more inventiveness in language, and more personal involvement.

In many ways, the structure of such a work borrows techniques that are used in fiction. A lively opening such as the one in "Captain Hind" seizes the attention of the reader. And after that it helps if you can create **dramatic questions**. We may suspect that Hind will lose in the end, but each clever escape provides a renewal of interest in the same way fiction often does.

Determining Your Tone

As I pointed out at the beginning of this chapter, Wedgwood takes the traditional approach to writing about history by not placing herself in the writing. She rarely uses "I"—in this little essay only once. But this doesn't mean that she maintains a strictly objective stance.

If you look at her phrasing carefully, you will see that she has an admiration for Captain Hind that she can't suppress. In the very first paragraph she indulges in her only use of "I" and establishes her fondness for the man:

> Highwaymen did not, as a rule, command the attention of the Government and I like to think that the dapper little man, as he entered on the last phase of his notorious career, had the gratification of knowing that he had achieved something.[6]

She continues to reveal her admiration in her phrasing. Hind, she tells us, "was the first to mark the profession with the strong imprint of his character." She follows this with a reference to "His gaiety, his daring . . . and elegant manners."

Later she pays another gentle tribute to him in this description: "Jemmy Hind was small and personable, with a confidence that did not overflow into swagger. . . ." An equally conscientious historian with a negative bias could have, using exactly the same sources, have written, "The pint-sized outlaw had a con man's confidence that approached a swagger."

In another descriptive sentence she writes, "Hind was a rogue but he was nature's gentleman." Again, it would not violate the historical record to write, "Hind was a habitual criminal with a pretense of civility."

As a final tribute, her last sentence concludes with the statement that his was "a death that many gentlemen had not been ashamed to die."

Literary treatment of history doesn't have to imply a partiality like this, but the genre provides that opportunity. While formal academic papers avoid biases (or bury them still deeper), literary nonfiction tends to present history with a more personal tone. Even when authors avoid the use of "I," they are free to reveal their feelings through the language they use.

---

[6]Renowned as Wedgwood is as a historian, she has her own laid-back approach to punctuation, especially with compound sentences. Fame has its privileges.

An Essay for Discussion

The concluding essay, "The Key," deals with relatively recent history and is based on personal experience.

It would be understandable if a discussion turned at least for a while to the social issues implied in this work: How far has our society come in civil rights in the past 50 years? What kinds of errors were made in the past, and how can we correct them? Where do we go from here? Important as these questions are, however, try not to lose sight of the essay as a sample of literary nonfiction. Here are some of the literary topics you might consider, either in your own review or in a group discussion:

Although the author's involvement is far greater in this essay than it is in many other historical pieces, the **narrator's** feelings—especially about his companions—are implied rather than stated. What are these feelings, and which specific details reveal them?

The door key is highlighted in the title and the concluding sentence. How is it being used? To what degree is that final question about the key encouraging or charged with uncertainty and frustration?

Are there any similarities between the use of the key and the jack-in-the-pulpit blossom as used in Clausen's essay?

The views expressed by members of the neighborhood, paraphrased from memory, suggest quite different responses to racial inequality. By chance, the sequence seems to echo shifts in attitude toward civil rights in the past few decades. See if you can identify them.

Finally, where is the line between essays that focus, directly or indirectly, on a period of history and those that are primarily expressions of opinion? Should there be a clear demarcation?

The Key

by Stephen Minot

The following account is factual. It happened on Albany Avenue in Hartford, Connecticut. The date was October 9, 1968. I have to state this clearly because it still seems more like fiction to me than a slice of history.

I don't mean to suggest that it was a dramatic event. We were three white guys trying to set up a street academy in a black neighborhood, and we didn't do very well. That simple. Neither the original effort nor the results were unusual. Objectively, the event was just a blip in the flow of history. No violence. No headlines. For me personally, however, the evening remains like an allegorical dream. The questions it posed are still not answered.

A friend of mine named David Colfax had called me up about two weeks before and filled me in on the details. He and a colleague, John Roach, planned to open a street academy in a minority neighborhood. So-called free schools had been established elsewhere with success, but none in that part of Hartford.

They had spent weeks looking for an available storefront and had finally located something satisfactory. They had signed a lease, mimeographed flyers, and found neighborhood supporters to publicize the first meeting.

The project would have sounded more promising two years earlier. After the assassination of Martin Luther King, Jr., black-white cooperation was at a low ebb. I had been through some bitter experiences. History seemed to be running against us. But I didn't have to tell Dave any of that. He had been through much more than I in the world of race relations. As a genuinely radical member of the Sociology Department at the University of Connecticut, he had been in the center of the black-white scene as well as the anti-war struggle. He had been honored by his draft board with a punitive re-classification to I-A at the age of 34 and, more recently, with a slanderous article devoted entirely to an attack on him in the *New York Times Magazine.* He was a veteran of good fights; I was in no position to remind him that war is hell.

The meeting was called for 8:00 p.m. at the storefront. The area was familiar to me. Albany Avenue had once been the border between black Hartford and white Hartford. Blacks and Puerto Ricans had spilled over into what was once the white side, so that by the late '60s it appeared to be wholly black territory, but everyone in the neighborhood still thought of it as the border.

It was an undistinguished, wide street dominated by used furniture stores, small markets, liquor stores, filling stations, and a few remaining apartments. Except for the eastern end, it was not a true slum.

You had to look carefully to see that it was once a white area. A few of the remaining meat markets still had Hebrew lettering on the windows; the furniture stores were without exception Jewish; and the liquor stores were mainly Irish and Italian. Most of those establishments had lost their plate glass in the riots after Martin Luther King's murder. Some were still boarded up.

The street still served as a kind of neutral ground between the two Hartfords, our own DMZ. A number of the Protestant churches there and at least one Catholic church were still manned by whites. Others had black ministers. They did their best to provide meeting space for groups trying to solve interracial and community problems. But the clergymen, both white and black, were in an awkward position. White radicals mistrusted them as cautious liberals, and blacks who attended such meetings ran the risk of being called *Tom.* The fictional Uncle Tom in Harriet Beecher Stowe's novel never struck me as a monster, but that's what he's become.

Colfax and Roach had tried for weeks to find a place not connected with a church, something in the "real ghetto" rather than on Albany Avenue, but partly because they were white and also because of the housing shortage they had to settle for this. It might have been an upholstery shop or a real estate office. It did not have a store-front window, and the three little glass panes in the door were small. One was covered by plywood. That would have advantages if there were more demonstrations, but it was no way to attract people off the street into a neighborhood free school.

When I arrived, Colfax and Roach were already there. They sat on one side of a scarred table. On the other side were two blacks chatting together, a man in a baggy sweater and a college-aged girl. There were also benches and an assortment of folding chairs but no one to use them.

We all nodded, but we remained like strangers in an elevator. I asked Dave how things were going in another battle he was involved in and he answered me briefly, but it was apparent to both of us that if we continued along those lines it would cut off the others and make this look like a white faculty club. So we dropped back to silence.

After a while a heavy, middle-aged black woman came in and eased herself down at the black side of the table, breathing heavily. It appeared that she didn't know anyone in the room.

"Well," John Roach said, as if we had all been waiting just for her, "I guess it's about time we got started." I looked at my watch and saw that it was already twenty minutes to nine. By my way of thinking, we were off to a very late start.

"We were hoping for a better turnout," he said. "We distributed over a thousand broadsides. But I guess we have a start here."

He then went on to describe what he and David had in mind. The University of the North End, it was to be called. An impressive title for those two shabby little rooms. I wondered how it would sound to the blacks. I wanted to ask, but John kept talking.

He didn't have any preconceived ideas, he said, but what they had planned were classes that would be relevant, subjects that would interest the people of the neighborhood, small classes, lectures and group discussions, seminar style. At first, we and some friends from the university would teach the classes; eventually members of the neighborhood would help out.

In all, he must have spoken for twenty minutes, ending with a reminder that it was their school and it was really up to them to make it work.

When he was through there was silence. We expected a discussion. This is what we were used to on our various campuses. But this wasn't a campus.

In the silence I noticed something I had only been subliminally aware of until now. About every five minutes there was a flash of light from the street. This time I turned in time to see through the dirty glass a slow-moving patrol car. His spotlight was trained on us. He must have been circling the block at walking speed ever since we had gathered. No one in the room paid attention.

Eventually John Roach broke the silence, telling them how badly he felt about there not being more neighborhood people there that night because this thing wasn't going to work unless the people in the area really felt that they owned it, ran it themselves. He developed this idea for another ten minutes or so. I had the uneasy feeling that I had wandered into an NAACP meeting of the previous decade.

The one-sided nature of the meeting was now so painfully clear that I had to interrupt my friend bluntly, speaking to the other side of the table: "So what's your reaction?"

Again there was silence. We strained against the compulsion to fill it. Finally the woman spoke up.

"Well," she said, speaking very deliberately, "what I want to know, is whether my boys would get credit. I mean, whether they could get credit, you know, so's they could get into a real college from here. That's what you need, credits. I got three young men and a grandson to raise. They'll be in trouble without more schooling, you know? What can this here school give them? That's what I'm wondering."

I think I saw Dave flinch. The neighborhood had just spoken, and what it was asking for was a return to the settlement house of the 1930s—the old ethnic escape hatch.

"Well . . . ," Dave said, using the cautious, infinitely patient tone I myself sometimes adopt when a student misses the entire point of the lecture, ". . . you see, we weren't exactly thinking in terms of credit. I mean, there are community colleges for that." And then he began to retrace what he and Roach had already covered.

About this time more neighborhood people began wandering in. A small flock of high-school girls, a young couple with a baby, three boys who might have been in the seventh or eighth grades, and a stray dog. As the door opened and shut, I saw that flash of light from the street. But still more people arrived. There was a certain amount of whispering and giggling, and the baby cried when the bottle slipped from his mouth. The dog scratched himself, his leg thumping on the floor. It began to sound like a viable neighborhood meeting.

John was in the middle of explaining to the newcomers what was involved in a neighborhood project like this. I heard him use the phrase "the pedagogical initiative" three times. As he rambled on, the rest of us began to notice that the man in the baggy sweater across the table had his hand up. He was not impatient about it. He was slouched forward with his elbows on the table, but one hand was raised, finger extended. There was no telling how long he had been sitting like that. "Hold it," Dave said, interrupting, pointing to the questioner.

"Yuh," the man said, lowering his hand. "Like, man, I've been listening, you know? Like I've been sitting here and listening, and I don't think you're getting it. I mean I really don't. Like, these cats are turned off on classes. They don't dig teachers, you know? I mean, like having one cat up at the head of the room, like, and him telling the others, 'Baby, you think it my way, cause that's the way it is.' I mean, you're not going to get cats in off the street for that. Folks around here won't have nothing to do with it. Oh, the ministers, maybe." There was a gentle chorus of "Yuh, man, yuh," from the back of the room which was now crowded. "Those Tom ministers. And they'll get some of their people down here. No hard feelings, but them Tom ministers will help you out because you're white, you know? They'll bring some people. Five. Six. Like you line them up and you learn them, but like who cares?"

At least the meeting had gone beyond the settlement house idea. He wasn't talking about credits and getting into white colleges.

"So what exactly do you want?" Roach asked.

"I mean, like some cat gets thrown out by the missus and he's on the street and the pigs they rough him up and tell him to get off the street and he comes in here. What's he want, a class about how to listen to Whitey's music?"

There was a ripple of laughter. We were on the defensive now. "So what do you want?"

"Well, he comes in here and he starts in about his missus and the pigs and how he feels about Whitey and there's other black cats here, and they start telling him about what black manhood is. They tell him how he don't take no pride in how he's black. They tell him, 'Shit, man, no wonder she threw you out. Like you're probably nothing but a Tom to her anyhow. An' no wonder the pigs pick you out—shuffling along like a Alabama nigger. You start thinking black, man, and you get support of the brothers, and the pigs'l think twice before they mess with you.' That's what we say to him. And we keep saying it. You know? Like night after night. An' maybe some day he gets a gun, see, and he kills that pig."

The time machine had spun forward again. This time there was real discussion. Some were against gun talk, some wanted classes in self-defense, some wanted to organize against the dealers. There was talk about rent strikes. We kept quiet, feeling very much in the minority.

More people arrived. A number of them were men in their early thirties and unattached. They had arrived together and I wondered if they had just come from some other meeting.

This particular group kept quiet through about 30 minutes of rambling discussion. And then one of them took over. He was lean, straight-nosed, and spoke with the slightly aristocratic lilt of a Jamaican. The Jamaicans had clout in Hartford. They even had their own cricket league. But what they were known for was political leadership.

"I just spent the summer out at Watts," he said. "And before that I was with SNCC in Georgia." There was total silence. He held the room in a way no one else there could. "And maybe you'd like to hear about what we're doing in Watts. I don't mean the government. I mean blacks."

He began outlining special neighborhood-run schools that neither followed the rigidity of public system nor gave in to the nondirective approach. Self-respect and community pride was at the heart of it. What the man with the sweater had been talking about in vague, intuitive terms, this man was able to describe as an educational system. He was tough, but there was no gun talk.

The meeting had spun down through the course of three decades and was on the very edge of being time-present. Turning at last to the local scene, he paused and looked at his audience.

"You want to get something going here?" he asked. "If that's what you want, start with your first set of classes next Monday. Leave the committee game to Whitey. Just start right in. And maybe you better have it strictly for blacks. You know what I mean?"

We all knew exactly what he meant. I had to remind myself that this was what we had hoped would happen. But this fast? With no planning? No money? With cops circling the place?

Still, it had happened, so one of us, Colfax, I think, said "So maybe you want to keep this meeting going without us being here."

He didn't have to ask. It was obvious. There was no outward sign of hostility. It was just that we had arrived at a certain point in history.

So the three of us got up and with difficulty threaded our way through what was now a crowded room. It was an awkward leave-taking. I longed for a handshake or even a nod of appreciation. We were on the same side, weren't we? But there was silence except for the scraping of benches and folding chairs. We hesitated at the door, but we couldn't think of any parting phrase. "No hard feelings" wouldn't have been entirely true; even "Good luck" might have sounded patronizing. We just left.

This had all happened so fast that we weren't sure how to react. Without speaking, we crossed the street and went into a little cafeteria which stood between two boarded-up stores. There were no other customers. We sat at a round table by the window and ordered coffee, which we certainly didn't need. The police car passed again, but the spotlight was on them, not us.

"Well, "Dave said dully, "I guess that's a great success."

"So why the depression?" John said, equally depressed.

"Well, it's not exactly the way we would have run it. I mean, does he really know what he's doing?"

"Who holds the lease?" I asked.

"We do."

"Maybe they could take it over."

He shook his head. "They couldn't pay the rent."

"You're going to pay it? Without even knowing what they're going to do with it?"

"We've got a choice?"

We sat in silence around that plastic-topped table and stared out across the blackness of Albany Avenue, the DMZ. It was late then. Trucks passed by and a few cars. The patrol car circled.

All we could see through the opaque glass pane in the door across the street were the backs of heads of those who were standing. There was no way of knowing what was going on or even who they were. Impossible to go back in. It was their meeting.

"Well," I said, "I guess it's time to go home."

Colfax shook his head. "Can't."

"How come?"

"We've got the key. How the hell do we get the key to them?"

• • • •

A

SUBMITTING WORK FOR PUBLICATION

Is it publishable? Compiling a submission list. Preparing the manuscript. Submitting a collection. Keeping records.

Is It Publishable?

Evaluating your own work is far from an exact science. If you are by nature an optimist, you are apt to submit work that doesn't have a chance for publication; and if you are a pessimist, you run the risk of never sending anything out. Whenever possible, rely on the opinion of others.

But not just anyone. If you are fortunate enough to have a friend who believes everything you write is brilliant, bask in the support but don't ask for advice. Instead, seek the views of those who read a good deal and are capable of judging your work with some objectivity.

If you are in a writing class, your fellow students will be a good source for criticism. As I have urged before, don't explain your intent in advance of a discussion and don't modestly apologize. Let them hear you read it or have them read copies before the class. Then listen without being defensive. When several members of a group feel that certain areas need work, take their opinions seriously. They are telling you that you will be wasting time and money by sending the work out before further revision.

Be realistic about the group. If all of you are just starting to write, it will be natural to evaluate each other's work relative to that of other beginners. Wild enthusiasm from fellow freshmen is good for morale but not a signal to send the piece out. If, on the other hand, you are in a class of experienced writers, some of whom have had publishing experience, you can assume that their view of excellence will be closer to that of publishers.

But what if no such group is available? How can you be objective about your own writing? One way is to compare what you feel is your best work with essays of the same type that are in print. If yours is a personal experience piece, see how it stands up relative to, say, three published works that are also autobiographical. They are not hard to find. The same is true of personal opinion essays, though remember that many of the letters to the editor of your newspaper are too pedestrian to be called literary nonfiction. You would do better to select models in magazines such as *Creative Nonfiction* or *Agni*. Additional magazine titles are listed in Appendix B.

It will be very difficult for you to compare your work with a variety of essays in print if you have not been reading literary nonfiction on a regular basis. The more you have read, the easier it will be to recall essays with a similar approach. Having back issues of magazines is extremely helpful. If you have adopted the routine of reading at least one or two short essays a day, consider keeping a list of works that impressed you, along with a notation of where and when they were published. If you record your thoughts in a personal **journal**, use that to keep track of your reading. The mind's retrieval system needs a backup.

Whatever your approach to evaluating your best work, select with care. Deciding to send out a particular piece means that you are prepared to make a sustained effort over a period of months, perhaps even a year or more.

Compiling a Submission List

Once you have made the decision that one or two of your essays are worth sending out, it is time to make a submission list. This is a list of four or more publications that might be interested in that particular essay.

Decide, first, which of three basic categories are appropriate for this particular piece: literary quarterlies (also known as little magazines), contests, or the **Op-Ed** pages of newspapers.

There are literally hundreds of little magazines in the United States, and selecting which will publish your kind of work can be daunting. You can find a good sampling of names and addresses in *Writer's Market* and a comprehensive list in *The International Directory of Little Magazines & Small Presses* (see Appendix B for details). The latter has an appendix listing titles by category such as such as satire, parenting, Buddhism, and geographic areas like California and New York. Don't forget, though, that many quarterlies that publish fiction primarily also accept nonfiction work.

It is essential that you then read sample issues in your library. Submitting "blind" (without firsthand familiarity) wastes time, postage, and the energies of hard-working editors many of whom are underpaid and overworked. Only by reading at least two issues can you be sure that they are on your wavelength.

Another reason for reading a publication before submitting is that many magazines (especially those listed in *Writer's Market*) are strictly commercial. Their quality may justify avoiding them.

Contests are listed in *Writer's Market* and often in *Poets and Writers Magazine* (see Appendix B), but select with care. Avoid those that offer a cash award without any mention of publication for the winner. The scam is simple: hucksters place ads for manuscripts and receive, say, 1,000 submissions, each accompanied by a "reader's fee" for $10. They select one (possibly without reading any) and send that person $500. The rest is their quick profit of $9,500. One such outfit repeats this every month in many different categories. It's legal but a sham.

If you do enter a contest, make sure that the winners' work will appear in a literary publication of merit. You can be sure that the reader's fee is justified since the magazine's reputation depends on the conscientious selection of winners. Make sure you have actually read that publication offering the award.

The third area to consider is the **Op-Ed** page of a newspaper. Names and addresses of newspapers can be found in *Literary Market Place*. Newspapers tend to prefer works of opinion and social commentary. Once again, make sure you have read sample issues. Your local paper may be a good start, but your library may subscribe to nationally known papers as well.

The reason you want to select at least four publications for your submissions list is psychological. Being rejected is a bit like being thrown from a horse. It's important that you get right back on. If you know exactly where the manuscript will go next, you can mail it out again on the same day it was returned. Don't give up until it has been to a dozen publications. Some writers up that to 20. Keep in mind that a work may be turned down for many reasons that have nothing to do with quality. The publication may be overstocked, it may have selected something similar the month before, or your first reader may have been in a foul mood.

Preparing the Manuscript

The mechanics are fairly standard. Set your margins so as to leave 1½ inches on the left and 1 inch for the other three sides. Editors prefer pica type, 10 cpi (characters per inch) throughout. (This is standard on most typewriters.)

About three inches down on the left type your name and address, single-spaced. Opposite that you can type "An essay," a word count, and your social security number, though this is optional. Two double-spaced lines below your address type your title. Use uppercase or lower, but never place the title in quotation marks and avoid a fancy font. Here is how it should look:

```
April N. Paris                      An essay
52 Ambition Ave.                    5,280 wds.
Middletown, IL 62666                015-42-3642

                    TRAVEL DREAMS
```

Now switch to double space. The first line of your essay starts two double-spaced lines down from the title. Avoid a justified (even) right margin. Leave it "ragged," as a typewriter does.

After the first page, type your last name and the page number on the upper-right corner like this (assuming you are Ms Paris): Paris 2, Paris 3, and the like. This is a safeguard in case the manuscript is dropped on the floor.

If anything is to appear in italics, indicate that by underlining. When you get to the end, just stop. "The End" is a mark of the amateur.

Why such an uncreative layout? Because your creativity should go into the essay itself, not the form. Tinted paper, flowers in the margin, and bizarre fonts are considered cute, unprofessional, and justification to stop reading.

Covering letter? Not unless you have something special to say. If the editor responded at all to an earlier submission, thank him or her briefly. Otherwise, just send the manuscript to a particular editor without comment.

Two more reminders: before sending the manuscript, proofread it twice more. Never rely on your spell check alone. It is unable to distinguish "to," "two," and "too," and accepts "it's" when what you meant was "its." This is clear proof that the spell check has a mental age of six. Some writers make a final check by reading each page from the bottom line to the top to prevent reading for content. It's your best way to pick up typos.

Is all this really necessary? Yes. Editors have to read hundreds of manuscripts; careless errors suggest that the writer didn't take the work seriously, so why should anyone else? A sloppy submission has two strikes against it after the first page.

The other reminder: enclose a self-addressed stamped envelope (**SASE**) for return. True, the postage is fast approaching the cost of another photocopy, but editors are used to receiving SASE's and are generally unwilling to type up an envelope even if it is only to send a rejection slip. Without SASE, you may never hear from them.

A few publications are beginning to accept work on computer disks, but make sure that they are willing to do so and can read your program. The endless and largely pointless upgradings of computer programs have increased corporate profits but have made it increasingly difficult to exchange disks.

Submitting a Collection

Collections are a group of short works by one author. Don't confuse them with *anthologies,* works by different writers. If you are just starting to write nonfiction articles, the question of whether to submit a collection of your own work won't concern you for a while. Wait until you have published 10 or more good essays.

For those close to that stage, however, here are answers to three of the most-asked questions:

1. *Should I consider working through an agent?* Literary agents are unlikely to be interested in handling single essays, but they are always on the lookout for promising collections. If your essays are in some way related and have been placed in well-known publications, it is well worth looking for an agent. But that may take time.

Start by asking for recommendations from friends who are familiar with agents. Lacking that, you can find names and addresses of agents in *Writer's*

Market or *LMP* (see Appendix B). Select about 10. Write individual but similar query letters to each of them. (This is perfectly acceptable since you are not actually submitting a manuscript.) Introduce yourself briefly (a paragraph); describe your collection (subject matter, not high self-praise) in two paragraphs. Close by asking if they would be interested in handling your collection. Enclose a one-page table of contents including where each piece was published. If you have other publications to your credit, enclose a separate bibliography or biography (one page). Some writers enclose a sample essay, though that is not essential. They'll ask for more if they are interested.

Of the ten agents you write, about three won't answer at all, and the rest will probably say "no" in varying degrees of courtesy. So select another ten. Tenacity is essential.

A reputable agent will submit your collection for you and will negotiate a contract in return for 15 percent of what you receive. Watch out for those who charge reading fees or submission fees.

Since finding a good agent may take time, consider submitting the collection yourself while continuing your search for someone to handle it. Even if you are lucky enough to receive a publisher's offer on your own, it would still be worthwhile to work through an agent. The fact that you already have a publisher interested will impress a potential agent.

2. *What kinds of literary nonfiction are most likely to interest a book publisher?* Reminiscences of dramatic childhoods are high on the list. By "dramatic" I mean being raised by parents who are famous, eccentric, or downright dysfunctional. Only a few writers are skillful enough to interest the public in a happy childhood. Another popular area is travel to unusual places in unusual ways—bicycle, on foot, on a camel. A third type consists of reflections composed in near-wilderness isolation, modern echoes from Thoreau's timeless *Walden Pond*.

3. *With or without an agent, what kinds of details should I look out for when negotiating a contract?* First, make sure that you understand the confusing clauses about electronic rights. This is still a new aspect of publishing, and some otherwise reputable publishers are taking advantage of it. A basic but unusually clear explanation is included in *Writer's Market* (see Appendix B). If in doubt, join the Authors Guild and ask for their advice about specific clauses. In addition, see if you can include a clause requiring acid-free paper. Acid paper is only slightly cheaper for the publisher and is presently destroying millions of books printed in the past half-century. Some publishers have a literary conscience and some do not.

Keeping Records

Some writers have convinced themselves that keeping records of their submissions is time-consuming and unnecessary, but neither is true. Here is a system that is simple and quick and will actually free your limited time for creativity. Buy a loose-leaf notebook. Assign a number to each essay you plan to submit, and write that number on the upper-right corner of a separate page. Use one line for each submission, recording the date of when you sent it, the publication, the editor, and the date you received it back. In the event that it is accepted, record that in red ink.

This may seem needless at first, but as soon as you start sending a number of essays, you will find it an invaluable system. It will keep you from submitting a manuscript to the same publication twice, will keep a record of any comment an editor may have added to a rejection slip, and eventually it will record your successes. There may even come a time when you will need that information for your tax returns.

B

RESOURCES FOR WRITERS OF LITERARY NONFICTION

Anthologies of literary nonfiction. Magazines that publish literary non-fiction. A sampling of booklength nonfiction. Books on writing techniques. Informational publications.

There is a hierarchy in the following five resource categories. I have placed lists of anthologies and magazines first and technique books toward the end for good reason. Now that you know what to look for, your development as a writer will thrive on reading essays themselves. Published writers of literary nonfiction stand ready to serve as your teachers. Think of them as members of the largest and most diverse university in the world. And the tuition is minimal.

Reading more about writing techniques, on the other hand, can reach a point of diminishing returns. The goal of any analytical text, this one included, should be obsolescence. Read it and move on. There exists a book club (not listed here) that offers a steady stream of how-to books on writing, but it seem unlikely that its subscribers will ever have time to write their own work. An aspiring violinist will not excel by staring at a succession of manuals, nor will a developing writer.

The benefits from reading depend not just on quantity but on quality and variety. For this reason, anthologies and magazines are the most valuable. Collections (works by one author) and book-length nonfiction works will be more valuable when you have become familiar with a wide range of short works by different writers.

Start by reading anthologies from your library. Buy those you want to keep and mark up. If your budget is tight, exchange them with a fellow writer, a two-for-the-price-of-one bargain. At the same time, subscribe to your choice of literary journals. They depend on you just as you as a writer depend on them.

Anthologies of Literary Nonfiction

The Eloquent Essay: An Anthology of Classic and Creative Nonfiction, John Loughery, ed. (Persea Books)

In Brief: Short Takes on the Personal, Judith Kitchen and Mary Jones, eds. (Norton)

In Short: A Collection of Brief Creative Nonfiction, Judith Kitchen and Mary Jones, eds. (Norton)

Roots and Branches: Contemporary Essays by West Coast Writers, Howard Junker, ed. (Mercury House)

Surviving Crisis: Twenty Prominent Authors Write about Events That Shaped Their Lives, Lee Gutkind (Putnam)

Writing Creative Nonfiction: The Literature of Reality, Gay Talese and Barbara Loundsberry (Addison Wesley Longman)

Magazines That Publish Literary Nonfiction

Atlantic Monthly, like *Harpers* (see below), is a monthly that features nonfiction. It also has some fiction, poetry, and reviews.

Harpers, similar to the *Atlantic* (see above). All four genres with emphasis on nonfiction.

Creative Nonfiction, a quarterly. All literary nonfiction. No ads, no fiction, no poetry. Good quality.

Georgia Review, a quarterly with a balance of genres similar to the *Virginia Quarterly Review* (see below).

Agni, published twice yearly. Includes fiction, poetry, reviews, and several nonfiction works each issue.

The New Yorker, a weekly. It publishes a story and a couple of poems in each issue, but it remains the most influential publisher of nonfiction. It was the first to print such momentous works as "The Silent Spring" and "Hiroshima." Major articles tend to be long and carefully researched. Others are short and humorous.

The New York Times Magazine Section, one of the few newspaper supplements that prints nonfiction with literary merit.

The Virginia Quarterly Review, a distinguished quarterly that publishes a balance of fiction, poetry, reviews, and nonfiction works of high quality.

A Sampling of Booklength Nonfiction

Assorted Prose, John Updike (Knopf)

Hiroshima, John Hersey (Random House)

In Cold Blood, Truman Capote (Vintage)

Iron and Silk, Mark Salzman (Random House)

Lives of a Cell, Lewis R. Thomas (Penguin)

The Lonely Other: A Woman Watching America, Diana Hume George (University of Illinois Press)

Remembering Heaven's Face, John Balaban (Simon & Schuster)

The Snow Leopard, Peter Matthiessen (Penguin)

Three by Annie Dillard, Annie Dillard (HarperCollins)
Walden and Other Writings, Henry David Thoreau (Bantam/Doubleday/Dell paperback)

Books on the Techniques of Nonfiction Writing

Art of Creative Nonfiction, Lee Gutkind (John Wiley)
Follow the Story: How to Write Successful Nonfiction, John B. Stewart (Simon & Schuster)
On Writing Well, William Zinsser (Harper)
The Travel Writer's Handbook: How to Write and Sell Your Own Travel Experiences, L. P. Zobel (Surry Books)
Writer Within: A Guide to Creative Nonfiction, Lary Bloom (Bibliopola Press)
Writing Creative Nonfiction: Instruction and Insights from Teachers of the Associated Writing Programs, Carolyn Forche and Philip Gerard, eds. (F & W Publications)
Writing the Memoir: From Truth to Art, Judith Barrington (Eighth Mountain Press)

Informational Publications

- *AWP Chronicle,* Tallwood House, Mail Stop 1E3, Fairfax, VA 22030-0079. Published by Associated Writing Programs six times a year in tabloid format. Articles, interviews, criticism, and news items about writers. Emphasis on poets and fiction writers, but also some on nonfiction writers. Information on creative writing programs, contest winners, and the teaching of writing. Circulation 13,000.
- *The International Directory of Little Magazines & Small Presses,* Dustbooks. By far the most inclusive listing of little magazines, quarterlies, literary journals, and small presses. It devotes a paragraph to each magazine, describing what it publishes and listing names of editors, payment scale, and the like. The appendix lists titles by subject, genre, and region. (Note: the categories entitled "Non-fiction" (sic.) and "Essay" do not include the many literary magazines listed under "Fiction" that also publish nonfiction.) Not included: large-circulation magazines, major publishers, and "how-to" articles. Strongly recommended.
- *Literary Marketplace,* R. R. Bowker Co. *LMP* does not list magazines, but it is the most authoritative annual listing of mainstream book publishers, literary agents, and writers' conferences. No articles on how to write or market your material. Cost: over $200, but most libraries have it.
- *The Writer's Handbook,* The Writer, Inc. An annual book with heavy emphasis on "how-to" articles. Focus is on commercial work, not literary writing. The list of literary magazines is less extensive than in *Writer's Market* and only a fraction of that in the *International Directory* (see above).

- *Writer's Market,* Writer's Digest Books, 1507 Dana Ave., Cincinnati, OH 45207. A slightly superior competitor to *The Writer's Handbook* (see above). Emphasis is also on commercial writing, but the list of literary journals is somewhat better. (Note: it includes a brief but invaluable explanation of electronic rights.)

- *Poets and Writers Magazine,* 72 Spring St., New York, NY 10012. A non-profit publication with emphasis on fiction and poetry but some articles and contest information on nonfiction. Published six times a year. Articles deal with problems faced by all literary writers: how to find time to write when teaching, how to arrange readings, publishing translations, dealing with small presses. Also a source of contest and grant application deadlines, dates of conferences and readings, and winners of awards. Circulation: 58,000.

- *The Writer,* 8 Arlington St., Boston, MA 02116. A monthly magazine with a heavy emphasis on mass markets. Articles on marketing a variety of material from gothic novels to "confessionals" and from poetry to greeting-card verse.

- *Writer's Digest,* 1507 Dana Ave., Cincinnati, OH 45207. Similar in emphasis to its competitor, *The Writer* (see above).

C

NOTES ON CONTRIBUTORS

Jack Bertram is a native Texan who lives in Mississippi. He is a newspaper features writer and a former road-paving superintendent. He received a master's degree from the Center for Writers, The University of Southern Mississippi. A poem of his that was originally printed in the *Mississippi Review* was reprinted in *Strong Measures* and later in *Three Genres*, 7th edition, both under the name of James Bertram.

Joseph E. Bruchac III is a Native American storyteller and writer who lives in the Adirondack Mountains region of New York state. He is the author of *Sacajawea, Between Earth & Sky* Harcourt Brace and, most recently, *Roots of Survival* (Fulcrum Press), among others.

Christopher Buckley is a widely published poet, essayist, and anthologizer whose poetry collections include *Fall from Grace* (BookMark), *Camino Cielo* (Orchises), *Dark Matter* (Copper Beech), and, most recently, *Appreciations*, a collection of reviews and essays. A native of California, he teaches at the University of California, Riverside, where he served as Chair of the Creative Writing Department.

Christopher Clausen is the author of *Faded Mosaic: The Emergence of Post-Cultural America* (Ivan Dee), *My Life with President Kennedy* (Univ. of Iowa), *The Moral Imagination* (Univ. of Iowa), and *The Place of Poetry* (Univ. of Kentucky). In addition, he writes regularly for *The American Scholar* and other periodicals. A Virginian by birth, he is currently professor of English at Pennsylvania State University.

Trinie Dalton is a high school English teacher. Her work has appeared in *L. A. Weekly, BOMB, Santa Monica Review,* and *Purple*. She lives in Los Angeles and is enrolled in the Bennington Writing Seminars MFA program.

Jodie Jackson Daviss has published both fiction (see *Three Genres*, 7th edition) and nonfiction. Her work has appeared in *Yankee, Story* and *Ambassador,* an in-flight magazine. She and her husband, a fellow writer, live in rural New Hampshire.

Tzivia Gover is a writer and editor whose work has appeared in the *Boston Globe, Poets & Writers Magazine,* the *Advocate,* and the *Christian Science Monitor,* among other publications. She received her master of fine arts degree in creative nonfiction from Columbia University.

James D. Houston lives in Santa Cruz, California. His publications include *Snow Mountain Passage* (Knopf), *The Last Paradise* (University of Oklahoma Press), and *The Men in My Life* (Capra Press), among others. His work has appeared in a number of publications including *Ploughshares* and *Zyzzyva.*

Stephen Minot has published three novels, including *Surviving the Flood* (Atheneum/Second Chance); two collections of stories, including *Bending Time* (Permanent Press); and three textbooks on writing. His fiction has been included in the *O. Henry Prize Stories* twice and *The Best American Short Stories* three times. He and his wife, *Virginia S. Minot,* a painter and printmaker, live in California and Maine. Virginia Minot's work appears on the cover of this volume and of *Three Genres,* 7th edition.

Marjorie Sandor's recent collection of essays is *The Night Gardener* (Lyons Press). Her collection of stories, *A Night of Music* (Ecco Press), won the Rona Jaffe Foundation Award for fiction. Her fiction and nonfiction have appeared in *Shenandoah* and the *New York Times.*

Gary Soto is a widely published Chicano poet, essayist, and fiction writer. His work includes *Poetry Lover* and *Nickel and Dime* (University of New Mexico Press), *A Natural Man, Junior College,* and *New & Selected Poems* (Chronicle Books.), and *Buried Onions* and *Jesse* (Harcourt Brace). He and his wife live in Oakland, California.

Destiny Ward is a biracial writer and student at Portland High School, Maine. Her articles have appeared several times in Portland, Maine, newspapers.

C. V. Wedgwood is a highly regarded British historian who studied at Oxford and also in France and Germany. Her specialty is the 17th century. Her works include *The Thirty Years War, Oliver Cromwell, The King's Peace,* and *Truth and Opinion* (Collins), which includes the essay "Captain Hind."

Connie Wieneke is a Wyoming resident who received her MFA degree from the University of Montana. She has published nonfiction, fiction, and poetry in a variety of journals including *Stand* and *Northern Lights.*

CREDITS

GLOSSARY-INDEX

This section can be used both for a quick review of literary terms and as an index. The definitions are limited to the ways each word is used in the text. Numbers refer to pages, and ff. means the analysis continues on the following page. Words in small capitals indicate a cross-reference in either the same or a closely related form; for example, IRONIC *is listed as* IRONY, *and* literature *is listed under* LITERARY WRITING.

Abstraction, 39, 103.   A word or phrase that refers to a concept or state of being. It is at the opposite end of a scale from *concrete,* words referring to objects we can see and touch. *Peace* is abstract; *dove* is a concrete word.

Ambivalence, 24, 64, 84, 118.   Contrasting emotions felt at the same time, such as love and hate, desire and fear. It may be expressed directly by a writer or revealed through action.

Base time, 30, 70, 86.   See FLASHBACK.

Biographical sketch, 7, 75ff.   A LITERARY NONFICTION essay that is FOCUSED on someone other than the author. The THEME may be CHARACTERIZATION (a picture of the individual as an end in itself) or some ABSTRACT concept such as dedication to teaching or self-centeredness.

Central concern, 20.   See THEME

Characterization, 76ff.   The technique of revealing character. It creates the illusion of having actually met an individual. Personal-experience essays may imply characterization through action and thoughts, though some reveal little about the writer. Characterization is usually stressed in BIOGRAPHICAL SKETCHES.

Character sketch, 7.   See BIOGRAPHICAL SKETCH.

Chronological, 29.   The presentation of events (usually in personal-experience essays and BIOGRAPHICAL SKETCHES) in the same sequence as they occurred in reality. It is opposed to nonchronological sequences, usually achieved through the use of FLASHBACKS.

Cliché, 107, 116.   A METAPHOR or, more often, a simile (see METAPHOR AND SIMILE) that has become so familiar that it no longer provides impact. "Good as gold," "neat as a pin," and "crystal clear" are true clichés. The word is also used to describe overused but nonmetaphorical phrases such as "tried and true," "each and every," and "last but not least." These are hackneyed phrases.

Concrete words, 39.   Words describing things that can be seen, felt, or, less often, heard, tasted, or smelled. Concrete words are at the opposite end of a scale from those that are ABSTRACT. "A rock" is unmistakably concrete; "writers" are less specific and so are midway on that scale; "immortality" is highly abstract.

Creative writing, 1.   See LITERARY WRITING.

Diction, 36.   The choice of words in any piece of writing. Diction is a significant factor in determining STYLE.

Dramatic question, 24, 31, 29. The emotional element in a LITERARY work that holds the attention of readers. An initial dramatic question is called a *hook,* but most works (especially those involving action) also provide a series of such questions to sustain interest.

Fiction, 1. Writing that tells an untrue story in prose. It may draw on people, places, or events in life, transforming them at will, but its only obligation is to the artistic creation. This is in contrast with LITERARY NONFICTION in which the writer assumes an obligation to be faithful to the actual people, places, and events he or she describes.

Figurative language, 39. See METAPHOR AND SIMILE.

Figure of speech, 39. See METAPHOR AND SIMILE.

Flashback, 30, 62, 69. The insertion of an earlier SCENE in any work that makes use of a sequence of events. The flashback departs from BASE TIME and normally (but not necessarily) returns to it.

Focus, 20. The primary subject matter or concern in a LITERARY NONFICTION essay. *Focus* is normally a particular person, place, or thing. It is contrasted with *theme,* which is the primary ABSTRACT idea suggested or implied by the work.

Formula, 13. See PLOT.

Frame story, 30. A story or nonfiction narrative in which the opening and closing scene occur roughly at the same time period and the rest of the PLOT occurs earlier. The major portion of the narrative is essentially one or more FLASHBACKS.

Genre, 1. Any of four basic types of literary or creative writing: LITERARY NONFICTION, FICTION, poetry, and drama. The term is also used, somewhat confusingly, to subdivisions of fiction such as "mysteries, "westerns," "Gothics," and "science fiction."

Hackneyed, 26. See CLICHÉ.

Hook, 25, 31. See DRAMATIC QUESTION.

Image, 103, 116. A word or phrase that can be perceived by one of the five senses. The most common are visual details. Images are CONCRETE as opposed to ABSTRACT.

Irony, 39. Verbal irony is phrasing in which the literal meaning is the opposite or significantly different from the intended meaning. Example: describing a hurricane as "a great day for a sail." It is similar to sarcasm, but doesn't have to be negative. Mild verbal irony takes the form of understatement as in the statement, "Picasso did all right as a painter." Cosmic irony (or irony of fate) refers to events that are the reverse of expectations such as a firefighter who dies from smoking in bed.

Journal, 4. A daily or fairly regular record of the writer's experiences, observations, and reactions to reading. It may be in a notebook or kept on a computer file. Entries are personal and informal, but some may serve as the basis of LITERARY NONFICTION or FICTION. *Journal* also refers to a literary publication, often a quarterly.

Literary nonfiction, 1. One of the four GENRES that constitute LITERARY WRITING. It is distinguished from the others by three basic characteristics: It is (unlike fiction) based on and is true to actual events, characters, and places; it is written in prose with a special concern for language; it tends to be more informal and personal than many types of nonfiction writing such as reports and research papers. "Literary nonfiction" is used interchangeably with "creative nonfiction."

Literary writing, 1. Works of poetry, fiction, drama, and nonfiction that use language artfully and develop insightful themes with some degree of sophistication. Such work is differentiated from light and sentimental verse, mass-market drama, and purely factual and utilitarian prose writing like reports, news items, and research articles. The term is used interchangeably with "creative writing." See also LITERARY NONFICTION.

Memoir, 6. A LITERARY NONFICTION essay based on personal experience. Characteristically, it is focused on events that occurred after a lapse of time such as reminiscences of childhood.

Metaphor and Simile, 39. A *simile* is a figure of speech in which one item (usually an ABSTRACTION) is compared with another (usually a CONCRETE noun) that is different in all but a few significant respects. The comparison uses "like" or "as." "He behaved *like a jackal* in Congress." A *metaphor* makes a comparison without using "like" or "as." The comparison is literally untrue but figuratively clear and vivid: "In Congress *he was a real jackal*." Don't confuse figurative language with a SYMBOL.

Modes, 37. See NARRATIVE MODES.

Narrative modes, 61, 130. The five methods by which a narrative (a sequence of events) in LITERARY NONFICTION or FICTION can be presented: dialogue, thoughts, action, description, and exposition. Most writers use all five to various degrees.

Narrator, 61, 130. In LITERARY NONFICTION the narrator is almost always the author. In rare exceptions, the bulk of an essay may be presented through the words of a witness or participant. Unlike in fiction, the narrator is never fictional.

Neutral style, 36. See STYLE.

Nonchronological, 29. See CHRONOLOGICAL.

Op-Ed, 15, 139. The section of a newspaper devoted to letters to the editor and personal opinion pieces from contributors. Though the views expressed are generally sincere and often forceful, almost none of the former and only a few of the latter can be described as LITERARY NONFICTION. "Op-Ed" is an acronym for "opposite the editorial page."

Overtone, 36. An additional meaning or meanings or qualities implied by a word or phrase.

Persona, 61, 62, 73. In FICTION, the NARRATOR of a story is to some degree invented and so is referred to as the "persona" to differentiate the character from the author. The term is rarely used in LITERARY NONFICTION because the narrator is almost always the author. In some cases, however, the author has insights at the time of writing that he or she didn't have as a younger person. In such cases, the subject of the essay can be referred to as the "persona." "Snakebit" by Connie Wienike (page 55) is an example.

Plot, 85, 102. A sequence of events in FICTION or in some types of LITERARY NONFICTION, especially personal experience and sometimes biographical sketches. It is usually divided into SCENES that may be arranged CHRONOLOGICALLY or nonchronologically. Plots that recur in fiction or film are called *plot formulas.*

Poetic, 34, 39. LITERARY NONFICTION (or FICTION) that is characterized by a STYLE that makes use of poetic devices such as METAPHORS, similes, SYMBOLIC language, and reflective passages.

Private symbol, 40. See SYMBOL.

Prose rhythms, 41. Rhythmical effects achieved in prose through repetition of key words or phrases or the repetition of sentence structure such as a series of questions or similarly phrased assertions.

Public symbol, 40. See SYMBOL.

Pun, 107. The use of a word or phrase in a way that emphasizes two different uses, or the use of two words that are alike or nearly alike in sound. It is often but not necessarily used in a humorous way. Most puns are essentially METAPHORS and so are a type of figurative language. In "Stone's Throw" (page 103), Jackson Jodie Daviss personifies a rock by suggesting that it "has undoubtedly held a series of steady positions."

Reflective essay, 8, 102. A discursive, thoughtful essay. It is usually less structured than an opinion piece and less concerned with events than a personal opinion essay. The THEME or themes of reflective essays are usually ABSTRACT.

Rhetorical question, 34, 41. A question asked, not to elicit information, but to achieve a stylistic effect or make a point. For example, "What could be better than a critic's unqualified praise?"

SASE, 140.   Self-addressed, stamped envelope. It is normally included with any submission of a work for publication.

Scene, 28.   A unit of action in a nonfiction work that deals with events—especially personal experience and character sketches. It may be defined by time ("The first time I met him . . . ") or by place ("The room was a total mess"), or even by TONE ("Whenever it rained I went into a deep depression"). It is a basic method of organizing such essays.

Simile, 39.   See METAPHOR.

Style, 35.   The manner in which a work is written. It is determined largely by the choice of words (DICTION), the type of sentence structure (SYNTAX), the relative use of NARRATIVE MODES) and the rate at which new information is revealed, and the TONE. *Neutral style* is that in which the style is inconspicuous.

Symbol, 40, 71.   An object, action, or state that is presented in a way that suggests a range of meaning larger than its literal meaning. *Public symbols* are widely known, such as the flag, the cross, Uncle Sam, and the like. *Private* (or *unique*) symbols are those devised by individual writers for a particular work. Examples in this text: in "Jack-in-the-Pulpit," by Christopher Clausen (page 65), the blossom that suggests "the abyss of death lying patiently in wait . . . "; and in "Stone's Throw," by Jackson Jodie Daviss (page 103), the rock that suggests immortality.

Synonym, 36.   A word that has the same or almost the same meaning as another word. In most cases, the meaning of the two words are not identical because of differences in the OVERTONES of each. "Car," "automobile," and "motor car" are synonyms, but each has a different set of overtones.

Syntax, 37.   Sentence structure; the arrangement of words in a sentence. It is one of the factors that determine the STYLE of a work.

Theme, 20, 78.   The primary statement, suggestion, or implication of a LITERARY work. It describes that portion of a work that comments on the human condition. Same as *central concern*. A literary work may contain several related themes.

Tone, 38, 129.   The emotional quality of a LITERARY work itself and of the author's implicit attitude toward the work as well. Some prefer to separate the two aspects of this definition, but most writers think of them as two forms of the same quality. Tone is described with adjectives like "exciting," "sad," "merry," "eerie," or "depressing," as well as "satiric," "sardonic," "ironic," and "dramatic."

Topic sentence, 95.   A sentence that introduces the subject of the paragraph that follows. Topic sentences occasionally appear within the paragraph or at the end. Such sentences are common in research papers but are also found in LITERARY NONFICTION.

Understatement, 106.   See IRONY.